What people are saying about
Evolutionary Metaphors

David Moore is one of a new generation of scholars inspired by the work of Colin Wilson (1931–2013). Assessments of Wilson to date, however, have concentrated on his early work as an existentialist philosopher, largely ignoring his later interests. In *Evolutionary Metaphors* David Moore takes as his focus Wilson's latter fascination with the 'UFO Phenomenon' as revealed in his 1998 book *Alien Dawn*. In so doing he provides a fresh and stimulating view of the work of one of the most fascinating and challenging authors of our time.
Colin Stanley, Author of *Colin Wilson's 'Occult Trilogy': A Guide for Students*, and Editor of *Around the Outsider: Essays Presented to Colin Wilson on the Occasion of His 80th Birthday*

Do flying saucers come from outer space, or the inner mind? In *Evolutionary Metaphors* David Moore brilliantly suggests they may originate in that strange liminal dimension that exists "betwixt and between"reality and dream, neither "inside" nor "out," which we know as the imagination. But what exactly is that? As Moore's hermeneutical journey reveals, it is nothing less than a mystery as mysterious as the UFOs themselves. Like a phenomenological man in black, Moore pursues abductor and abductee, and finds that the evidence for extraterrestrials poses some fundamental questions about reality itself. No spacecraft required. Reading this alone will take you out of this world.
Gary Lachman, author of *Dark Star Rising: Magick and Power in the Age of Trump* and *Beyond the Robot: The Life and Work of Colin Wilson*

T0163033

Evolutionary Metaphors

UFOs, New Existentialism and the Future Paradigm

Evolutionary Metaphors

UFOs, New Existentialism and
the Future Paradigm

David J. Moore

BOOKS

Winchester, UK
Washington, USA

First published by O-Books, 2019
O-Books is an imprint of John Hunt Publishing Ltd., 3 East St., Alresford,
Hampshire SO24 9EE, UK
office1@jhpbooks.net
www.johnhuntpublishing.com

For distributor details and how to order please visit the 'Ordering' section on our website.

ISBN: 978 1 78904 087 6
978 1 78904 088 3 (ebook)
Library of Congress Control Number: 2018938716

A CIP catalogue record for this book is available from the British Library.

Design: Stuart Davies

UK: Printed and bound by CPI Group (UK) Ltd, Croydon, CR0 4YY
US: Printed and bound by Thomson Shore, 7300 West Joy Road, Dexter, MI 48130

We operate a distinctive and ethical publishing philosophy in
all areas of our business, from our global network of authors to
production and worldwide distribution.

Contents

Introduction

The enormous range of UFO literature can leave one feeling baffled and discouraged, particularly as its size is often only equalled by the absurdity of its contents. This is an unfortunate situation, for what it is attempting to address ought to be taken very seriously. Now, it was in this spirit of confusion—and discouraged by many of the blind alleys—I turned to Colin Wilson's 1998 *Alien Dawn* as a guidebook to the subject's unpredictable terrain.

At this point I had already read his earlier *The Outsider* (1956), a clarifying criticism of the cul-de-sac that existentialism had led itself into, while providing a great synthesis of a wide variety of writers, thinkers and artists who had also grappled with the mysteries of existence. Wilson was able to provide an optimistic advancement of a difficult subject, providing a way out of the maze of nihilism and pessimism that had plagued existentialism for decades. So, it seemed to me that *if anybody* had the intellectual tools necessary for illuminating the complex mystery of the UFO phenomenon, with sympathy and intelligent sensitivity, it would be found in Wilson's 'bird's-eye view' survey of the subject.

After setting down the foundations for his life's work with *The Outsider*, it was clear that whatever Wilson was to undertake would be implicitly carrying this 'new existentialist' banner towards an enlargement of our understanding of man's existential predicament. There was, as many readers recognised, an evolutionary directive in his work which aimed to unveil the essential *meaning*, or evolutionary purpose, inherent in any pursuit or idea. That he had an insatiable drive towards the understanding of human existence, in its widest sense, is supported by his fearlessness in aiding in the publication of Ian Brady's *The Gates of Janus* (2001). A highly controversial move, but which nevertheless presented a unique and invaluable contribution to our understanding of criminal psychology. Therefore, Wilson, for me and many others, came to represent a fearless explorer of the dark and occulted recesses of the human psyche, but significantly, *without a pessimistic bias*.

Wilson's approach to ufology retained this evolutionary spirit, for he asked the essential question: 'What can it tell us about ourselves, our consciousness?'—a question informed by the philosophical discipline of phenomenology, which aims to reveal the mechanisms of man's psyche, and its dynamic and interpretative role *through man* and towards reality.

Now, the mystery and mythology of extraterrestrial intelligence is essentially driven by an attempt to catch a glimpse into an alternative state of consciousness; it even suggests a new approach to existentialism, the problem of terrestrial and non-terrestrial existence. This is at the heart of Ian Watson's superb novel, *The Embedding* (1973), which is about how extraterrestrials process—through the medium of language—reality and meaning. Indeed the extraterrestrial, as an idea and/or reality, presents a phenomenological mirror which simultaneously distorts and illuminates man as he sees himself in relation to the cosmos. There are of course many shifts in perspective involved: philosophical, psychological and cosmological, with its many other concomitants such as history, culture and the rise of science. Moreover, mankind, the most self-aware creature that we know of, has no other cultural or existential referent except of those evolved on Earth. As I have said, the extraterrestrial, by default, represents a new type of existentialism, and it could be argued that science fiction may become the preparatory groundwork for contact with different forms and new 'modalities' of being. One could argue that the alien may represent man as *abstracted to himself*—or, as Stan Gooch proposed, as a part of 'the on-going folklore' of the Ego. Science fiction, then, becomes the avant-garde of this evolving folklore.

Alien Dawn is a comprehensive summary of both the

experience itself and the literature that attempts to peel away at the phenomenon's persistently mercurial character. Towards the end of the book, in a chapter significantly titled 'The Way Outside', Wilson attempts his 'bird's-eye view': a sort of grand synthesis of the subject's possible meaning. For this he calls upon the frontiers of contemporary science, along with developments in parapsychology, cosmology and philosophy. Indeed, it is clear by the title of this chapter that Wilson was attempting to find a 'way outside' the entanglement of absurdity and paradox that surrounds ufology (to both researcher and witness alike). Now, what is unique about this is how Wilson drew upon science fiction—particularly Ian Watson's *Miracle Visitors* and even the late Brian Aldiss' short story 'Outside'—to stretch the contextual boundaries of our understanding of the phenomena; throwing open new and *imaginative* approaches to a phenomenon that baffles and frustrates the rational intellect. It was this element of *Alien Dawn* that provided a refreshing interpretation of a phenomenon that tirelessly weaves itself through riddles and contradiction.

As one nears the end of Wilson's book a pattern finally emerges, for Wilson's allowance of the imagination in the phenomenological arsenal enables one to grapple more actively with the categorical mechanisms of consciousness itself; those mental blinkers that the UFO appears to utilize like a chameleon. There is a sense that in imaginative literature, the perceptual speed and flexibility is up to the task of revealing a facet of the mysterious reality *behind* the phenomena it attempts to imagine. In other words the imagination, as well as imaginative literature, informs us far more about our reality than we realise.

There is an element of farce at the heart of ufology and the UFO-experience, and it is what Wilson called the problem of 'deliberate unbelievableness'. Wilson's biographer Gary Lachman, in *Beyond the Robot: The Life and Work of Colin Wilson* (2016), even remarked that one begins to wonder if these extraterrestrial beings—commonly associated with UFOs—are 'fans of Monty Python, the Marx Brothers, and the Three Stooges.' Lachman goes on to say that this might be a deliberate attempt to frustrate our interpretations; forcing us out of our perceptual laziness. One could say that the phenomenon invites an active, vigilant, rational as well as imaginative character for its interpretation. In this sense, the UFO phenomenon offers itself up as a pedagogical tool: a deliberately obscure and frustrating code that haunts the most obsessive cryptographer. To a receptive and open mind the mystery that the UFO represents demands an explanation, but, with an unduly dismissive or lazy mind, this will not be forthcoming. The phenomenon persists in spite of this, and only a few take the time to consider its nature. Nevertheless, there have been many brilliant attempts to unravel this mystery, with the work of Jacques Vallée, John E. Mack, and the more recent work of Jeffrey Kripal and Jason Reza Jorjani, developing a more hermeneutical and phenomenological approach to the subject.

All of these individual approaches have included the active mode of interpretation, reaching a balance somewhere between what Carl Jung called 'active imagination' and a philosophical and scientific rigor. All of the above writers have acknowledged the importance of the *act of interpretation itself* as being a significant component in the reciprocation of our understandings, both presented and re-presented, and both theoretically as well as experientially (as in the case of abductees like Whitley Strieber, for example).

If there is indeed some reality to the phenomena, as seems to be the case, then it demands to be seriously scrutinized; and, as the field is still in its early developmental stages, an imaginative approach is as good as any for grappling with its mystery, for ambiguity seems to be the phenomenon's element. Someone well acquainted with hallucinogenic logic, Terence McKenna, even went so far as to suggest that the UFO is a gauntlet thrown at the feet of scientists—a sort of 'crack this!' puzzle. Furthermore, the mystery appears to conceal something valuable—or at least, it taunts us into an imaginative interpretation, 'presencing' itself between fact and fiction, existing as a sort of 'conceptual caricature' of our culture's blind spot. One comes away after reading much of the literature with the nagging suspicion that somewhere along the line we missed *the point*, rather like failing to grasp a Zen kōan—the very reason for its clownishness is because we are only aware of half the picture.

Now, Wilson, in *Alien Dawn*, at least provided a context big enough to grapple with at least some of its implications, pointing towards several 'ways out' of the maze of absurdity and towards a more integrative understanding—both of the phenomenon itself and ourselves.

To use the phraseology of Professor Jeffrey Kripal, Wilson was able to 'make the cut between "what appears" and "what is"' (2016: 45). In other words, Wilson was able to switch between the two, and simultaneously acknowledge the bit 'in-between'; the occulted 'middle-way' between Being and *the meaning content of the experience itself*. It is, as Wilson recognised, a perceptual phenomenon as well as an objective event—the inside-out 'seamlessness' where the two become indistinguishable. Now, imaginative speculation (drawing upon science fiction, for example, or relying on intuition) is discouraged in science and, of course, it is not an effective point from which to set our epistemological foundations. Yet it is intimately involved in our ontological reality, and this is what phenomenology acknowledges insofar as it is concerned with reality *as a whole*; by including both seer and seen. Implicit in phenomenology and Wilson's 'new existentialism' is an acknowledgement of this 'occulted bridge' which includes what we might call 'the other half of reality'.

All this was recognised by the Harvard psychiatrist, John E. Mack, who, being one of the few practitioners to listen to the witnesses and abductees on their own terms, accumulated and cross-referenced much anecdotal material to confirm to himself and others that there is indeed some existential referent to these accounts. Anyone who reads his 1994 book *Abduction* will come away convinced of the internal consistency to many of the reports, and feel that it is unlikely that everybody is making up the same—and to no evident advantage to themselves—often absurd story. In other words, Mack felt that the phenomenon ought to be treated as many of the witnesses themselves treated it. That is, as an apparently objective phenomenon insofar as they have had a genuine effect on the psychology of the individual—therefore recognising that something 'real enough' was experienced. They were, Mack concluded, relating a version of the truth *as they saw it and as they experienced it*, often finding it an extremely difficult and traumatic experience to recall, let alone understand. For Mack it was not entirely an intrapsychic event, but an open assault on our dualistic borders of mind/body, real/unreal and so on.

Furthermore, as an idea the UFO and its interrelated subjects—alien abduction, implants, cattle mutilation, extrasensory perception and occult knowledge—have been effortlessly absorbed into the science-fiction imagination. Indeed, the origin of the experience itself is so deeply entangled with our cultural entertainments and mythologies that it is difficult to locate the *origin* of the experience, and how its cultural ambience shapes the witnesses' interpretation of events subjectively. Again this is something that the phenomenon seems to exploit, which suggests that it is (A) *located in the individual's imagination* and therefore is a mixture of cultural mythology and personal delusion; (B) an emergent presence, as such, from the collective unconscious of mankind's shared mythological imagination; or (C) an objective-subjective (what Michael Talbot calls 'omnijective') phenomenon that exists—or blurs the dividing lines—between what is ordinarily perceived and experienced as fundamentally separate, either/or. The notion of 'either/and', of course, would mean a combination of all three examples of its possible origin.[1]

If this is the case, one may approach the problem, which initially appears as insoluble, with a type of contextual 'playfulness' in which one shifts the various arrangements to see if anything *new* emerges from the apparent chaos. We have to be as swift and as versatile as the trickster at the heart of the phenomenon. Indeed, the field of ufology, with its bold contexts, unusual statements, witnesses of the otherworldly, and so on, presents itself as a field rich with—and even prone to—imaginative speculation. It is the stuff of fantasy and of 'boldly going where no man has gone before'. Of course, our speculation should not dispense with the 'facts' at hand, but instead have as its goal an *integrative* context that might provide an answer by reining in as many approaches as we can marshal. A working towards a new approach ought to embrace a certain amount of experimentalism if it is to incorporate a flexible enough structure—and like physical explorers, mental explorers should distinguish between fact and fancy in this strange world of new and exotic laws. It may be that with an effective and sensible use of our imagination, we might acquire the essential puzzle piece that generates the most useful gestalt from the sum of the phenomenon's difficult parts.

This essay is an attempt at such a gestalt. By attempting to pull together as many ideas as possible one might find a 'way outside' the phenomenon, and in doing so one might hope to glimpse an outline of some of the laws which underlie occult phenomenon—rather like the traveller in Flammarion's famous 1888 engraving in which a man peers behind the veil of ordinary reality. If the UFO itself has a 'bird's-eye view' of *us*—both figuratively and literately—we, in turn, have to rise above *its* logic to see, in turn, how and why it functions the way it does. We might call this either a search for super-consciousness or 'UFO consciousness', but as I suspect that the UFO experience is *both a metaphor towards a new understanding of reality*, it might be interpreted as I have attempted in this essay: as an *evolutionary metaphor*.

An approach that incorporates metaphor, imagination and ideas pertaining to the evolution of consciousness requires a high degree of comparativism and analogical thinking. It also requires one to temporarily abandon or re-examine 'fixed theories' — without leaving them too far from hand—crystallizations that may either prove advantageous or inhibitory to our larger understanding. Ufology, a relatively new discipline, is not immune to such internal limitations but—and by its very nature—it tends to spread like an ink blot over multiple other interrelated fields. Contradictions and absurdities abound, for as soon as one settles on any 'given', there arrives another case which frustrates and undermines any such theoretical structure that was initially established. This is a very common occurrence, for example, in crop-circle research, in which frauds and 'real' circles become intermixed; on top of that is the 'human element', where the mystery and the 'truth'—whatever that might be—is deliberately obscured. As well as these internal problems within the field (crop fields or ufology), there is also the fact that it is treated as a cultural backwater. It is essentially perceived as a thankless task based on a lie, and generally undertook by cranks expressing themselves in what, for most, is an alien language in itself. Furthermore, the only other disciplines or systems of knowledge that can tackle its conceptual enormity are ironically similarly 'rejected': esotericism, parapsychology and the difficult—yet increasingly growing—bridgehead of spirituality into quantum physics.

There is no 'Tao of ufology' or an all-encompassing 'theory of everything'.

To place these theoretical and historical difficulties aside, we may want to turn to the sky itself, and reflect on the fact that it is both symbolically and truly a vision into an unidentifiable mystery. Our moon, for example, is instantly identifiable—few have even travelled to and from it—but still, anything that exceeds beyond it remains difficult for our instruments to explore. And then, beyond a certain limit, it is again *unknown*. We cannot, for better or worse, 'correlate all its contents', as the horror writer HP Lovecraft celebrated of the mind itself. Furthermore, our manifest universe is the backdrop of our cosmologies and our imaginative projections—our 'What ifs?'. Indeed, from religion to genres of speculative fiction, we populate the regions of the unknown with divine personages or other beings like or unlike us. What *haunts* this mysterious space is psyche, of mind and its illuminations, and this is a part of an ancient tradition, sometimes symbolised as Isis' star-clad veil—and sometimes 'unveiled' by acclaimed or condemned occult adepts.

Leonardo da Vinci wrote a defence of this attentive gaze into the manifest cosmos, for he saw it as the basis of creativity, and moreover an ability to perceive new forms usually obscured from our ordinary perception. This imaginative engagement with the world may explain his extraordinary creativity and visionary powers, so it is therefore instructive for anyone pursuing the fruits of imagination to understand this method of active imagination, for this may prove indispensable in our integration and understanding of some of the stranger phenomenon that we shall encounter. Here da Vinci describes his curious method:

> If you look at any walls spotted with various stains or with a mixture of different kinds of stones, if you are about to invent some scene you will be able to see in it a resemblance to various different landscapes adorned with mountains, rivers, rocks, trees, plains, wide valleys, and various groups of hills. You will also be able to see divers, combats and figures in quick movement, and strange expressions of faces, and outlandish costumes, and an *infinite number of things which you can then reduce into separate and well conceived forms* [my italics].[2]

This type of thinking, a sort of psychological and creative form of gestalt, has gained popularity in more recent times and has particularly been adapted into a contemporary form of magical theory and practice called 'chaos magic'. A brief comment on the subject will prefigure some of the ideas that I will pursue in this essay, and so it is to one of the founders of chaos magic, Peter J. Carroll, that we shall pay particular attention. Apophenia, or indeed, pareidolia, is a creative perceptual act that transposes—or brings forth—meanings and patterns out of apparently chaotic or highly complex situations, images or thoughts. In other words, anything that has implicitness (a poem for example) is open to an interpretation—or hermeneutic 'reading'—in which the observer is inextricably a part. The poem without interpretation, of course, would only exist in a flux not unlike the cat in Schrödinger's famous thought experiment— suspended in a hypothetical betwixt state of either/or until it is 'collapsed' into *isness* by the act of observation. Both apophenia and pareidolia are essential to the psychotherapeutic discipline of gestalt therapy, which begins from the principle that man has a 'meaning faculty' that grasps totalities—that his consciousness is naturally connective rather than deductive. In other words, perception aggregates 'parts' into 'wholes' in the same way a baby recognizes his mother's *whole* face almost instantaneously. Not by an act building up an image bit-by-bit but by an unconscious mechanism that collates the sum of the parts, thus resulting in the near miraculous recognition of pattern, form and, importantly, *meaning*.

Carroll goes on to say in *The Apophenion* (2008) that these traits can be found particularly amongst 'magicians, mystics and occultists'; however, it also affects many individuals who often provide advances, more generally, in other less 'magical' endeavours by their sheer creative drive. Invention is basically where the imagination converges with an objective reality, in which the imagined thing is amenable to the laws of objective reality. When this happens the imagined form takes shape in the world of space and time, and is palpable and functional as either an object, or as a symbol of higher truths, providing a sort of 'bridge' between the two worlds. It is as da Vinci said, a 'well conceived *form*'. Creativity of this kind is crucially important for a culture's health, and also presages scientific advances that are enormously beneficial.[3] Pareidolia, similarly, works by associations and 'map making' projections through which man can begin to see elephants in clouds, astrological parallels, and even hysterical conspiracy theories entirely divorced from reality. Carroll certainly acknowledges these psychological dangers of unbridled 'meaning perception',[4] but he argues quite convincingly that these very perceptual abilities play a significant part in 'the development of art and religion' (2008: 8).

Chaos magic is perhaps the most contemporary and explicit example of a theory of the imagination and its power, for it is particularly orientated towards its application both creatively and magically. Later on in this essay I will draw upon some of its other aspects and limitations in a larger context. Chaos magic is basically a scaffolding of a system that recognises the value of phenomenology. Again, its logic points towards an active use of imagination in the study of mind and reality. Metaphors, which become magical 'sigils' within chaos magic, are used as bridges into new associations, and ways of seeing novel potentialities.

Wilson, both anticipating chaos magic and honing his own phenomenological approach, states in *Beyond the Outsider*: 'The world seems to be wearing a mask, and my mind seems to confront it helplessly; then I discover that my consciousness is a cheat, a double agent. It carefully fixed the mask on reality, then pretended to know nothing about it' (1965: 93). With the mercurial world of imagination and the UFO phenomenon, this is wise counsel when dealing with the 'double agent' of the mind and its powers; especially considering both our own and the phenomenon's ambiguous relationship to reality—objective or subjective.

The trajectory of this essay from here on is similar to that expressed in Wilson's fifth book of the Outsider Cycle, *Origins of the Sexual Impulse* (1963), in which he outlines two ways of going about analytical writing:

> One is to define all of your terms with scientific precision... and then stick closely to those definitions throughout. The other is to rely on your reader's instinct and common sense. All originators in philosophy are forced to rely on the second method (because so much of their work depends on intuition)... Any professional writer — that is, any writer who is concerned about direct communication with his reader — will certainly be inclined to prefer the 'intuition' method... (1970: 15)

I intend to proceed in the spirit of Wilson's 'intuition method', using what Lachman calls an 'intuitive glue' to piece together the many fragments of ufology. It is worth emphasising again that ufology is a relatively young field that is in the process of substantiating its presence as a serious area of study.

Here it is my contention that the UFO, by being as ambiguous as it is, is a deliberately mystifying 'presence' that affects the structures of that mercurial world of Carl Jung's collective unconscious. Myths, if they have any substantial foundations in true events at all, may be that which aggregate around an initially information-rich bafflement of the senses (of the individual or the target society). Religions are perhaps the structures that emerge to 'explain away' the initial phenomena of the miraculous — that is, they are stories which absorb the 'shock' into a comprehensible and pedagogic narrative. Referring as they do to something beyond the scope of ordinary language, the stories are necessarily metaphorical, that is, inferring something beyond the limitations of ordinary language. Visionary art, emerging from the powerful and tumultuous depths of subjectivity, nevertheless present to us something hauntingly objective. It is this art that stands the test of time for its undeniable truth value, with its enormous poignancy stimulating our recognition of profound depths of meaning. Meaning on the threshold of what is ordinarily expressible or even comprehensible.

We may ask, with some speculation, *what the UFO teaches us* — if anything — about the creative matrices underlying the evolution of human consciousness. Is this phenomenon *outside* of us, or is it, perhaps, a type of 'bootstrapping paradox' involved with mankind's own self-evolution? As we shall see, these questions develop exponentially, and before we know it we are back into the domain of common existential questions, albeit with an evolutionary beckoning.

Life, according to Wilson, works in 'terms of symbols and language' and when the 'flame of consciousness is low, a symbol has no power to evoke reality, and intellect is helpless' (1966: 112). In this essay I have taken the symbol of the evolution of human consciousness as a possible solution to the enigmas that the UFO represents. Its presence, I believe, fits into a general philosophical bracket of the 'evolutionary metaphor': that playful extrapolation of something beyond the ken of ordinary perception. William James once said that there can 'never be a state of facts, to which new meaning may not truthfully be added,' that is *'provided the mind ascend to a more enveloping point of view.'* But it is also worth keeping in mind Carl Jung's dictum that the 'highest truth is one and the same with the absurd', for in ufology, as in life, the two often converge when the flame of consciousness is burning bright.

This essay represents my own attempt to continue in the spirit of where *Alien Dawn* left off, and it is also my own endeavour to throw some auroral illumination into this phenomenological twilight zone.

The Power of the Question

Contradictions abound in many of the 'explanations' for the UFO phenomena. The field is simply too complex and ever-changing; even transitional with its leaping developments and evolution as a phenomenon. To pull back, so to speak, and gain a 'bird's-eye view' requires both a familiarity with the literature and a mind tempered by philosophical rigor as well as sympathy— even patience—towards the uncanny and unusual. As I have mentioned above, any young discipline that hastily settles on an all-encompassing theory, the sooner it finds itself contradicted, inconsistent. The sheer flow of information, of emerging evidence and mounting witness accounts, is almost consistently churning up even the firmest of theoretical foundations. These elements are not necessarily the fault of ufology and its individual researchers; indeed *it is an issue that the phenomena itself appears to exploit.*[5]

There is a persistent ambiguity latent in the UFO 'presence', and any theory that can preserve its credibility requires itself to be constantly updated, vigilant and flexible enough to allow the field to swiftly evolve in tandem with the phenomenon itself. Again, it is important to note that the phenomenon *evolves and develops*, and it is not a static mystery but a dynamic enigma. It is towards a general widening and complexity which will allow ufology the freedom and innate flexibility to fully establish its foundations in a field that shifts beneath it—but first, one has to survey the terrain before he begins construction.

The Super Natural (2016)—a collaboration between Whitley Strieber, an abductee and horror novelist, and Professor Jeffrey Kripal, a specialist in philosophy and religious thought— reads at times like a hybrid of Wilson's *Introduction to the New Existentialism* (1966) mixed with a mystical commentary on the shadowy realms of esotericism and depth psychology. Kripal describes the discipline of hermeneutics—the central theoretical approach which runs throughout the book (although mainly in Kripal's own responses to Strieber's autobiographical material)—as 'the art of interpretation that deciphers the hidden meanings of some enigmatic symbol, text, dream, vision, or striking coincidence' which, he states, recognises 'a single process that co-creates both the subject and the object *at the same time*' (2016: 112–113). Again, we are back to Wilson's notion that consciousness is a 'double-agent'.

The trickster god Hermes, whose name constitutes the very word 'hermeneutics', has been called by Jorjani an archetypal 'dialectical antagonist',[6] a sort of 'living' kōan of the collective unconscious. The 'hidden meanings' of these symbols reveal a radically new understanding of our ontology, that is, they present evolutionary metaphors concerning our state of being, and how we attend—through our intentionality—in an active participation between the world of phenomenon and our selfhood. The UFO, for Strieber, Kripal and Wilson, is such a symbolic reality—a simultaneous co-creation of the trickster double-agent and our own inner dialectical antagonist.

Now, one of the common myths within ufology is that these sightings began as a sort of Cold War hysteria, a mass psychic product born from geopolitical tension. Carl Jung even speculated along these lines in his book *Flying Saucers* (1958). And although Jung's book goes a lot further than this 'Cold War hypothesis', it is strange that some sceptics regard Jung's explanation as an all-encompassing answer to the problem, a sort of 'explaining away' a phenomenon by reducing it to a psychic compensation mechanism of collective trauma. Indeed, Jung's work is perhaps one of the more intelligent and academic contributions to ufology; sadly, however, it has come to be as misunderstood as the phenomenon it attempts to analyse. What is often overlooked is the fact that Jung is interested in the very concept of a UFO—that is, as a possible incursion of extraterrestrial or inter-dimensional entities within our skies and psyches—and considers how our minds might react to such strangeness. Jung goes on to say that our:

> [...] conscious mind does not know about them and is therefore confronted with a situation from which there seems to be no way out, *these strange contents cannot be integrated directly but seek to express themselves indirectly*, thus giving rise to unexpected and apparently inexplicable opinions, beliefs, illusions, visions and so forth [my italics]. (2002: 7)

This 'indirect expression' of the phenomena is central to this essay, for the UFO 'presence' appears as a sort of drama, a symbol, within a self-mythologizing sequence of events calculated by some playwright of the absurd and uncanny. An indirect form of expression is also a common hallmark of the evolutionary metaphor. It is important to remember the apparently *deliberate strangeness* of such experiences—or, moreover, the enigmatic resonance of the event that distorts our perceptions of the phenomenon. This, importantly, is acknowledged in both Kripal's and Jorjani's hermeneutic and phenomenological method of analysis.

An example of *deliberate strangeness*: one female witness once reported that she saw a 'fifteen-foot kangaroo in a park, which turned out to be a small spacecraft' (Mack; 1994: 396). In short, one could say this is truly mercurial; it abides by the principles of the trickster, even that of a satirist of public opinion. In their transitional existence 'betwixt-and-between' they act—as Victor Turner says in his study of the notion of liminality, *The Ritual Process* (1966)—in a way to provide a 'generative' as well as 'speculative' tendency in the individual or society which attempts an understanding of the mysterious, that intermediate 'other'. Importantly Turner concludes by saying that the 'mind that enters willingly will proliferate new structures, new symbols, new metaphors' (quoted in Hyde; 2008: 130). Nevertheless, its resonant absurdity remains, and its interpretation turns our usual sense of reality inside out.

It is this place betwixt-and-between that is represented in the Kabbalah as the fertile egg of chaos; the origin of new forms and the place where the implicit and explicit are inverted, seamlessly swapping places. It is also the domain in which apophenia and pareidolia come as compensatory tools, reordering our senses, generating new patterns and meanings which take root, or even drift away and back into the tumultuous churn of *potentia*. This is the essential 'stuff' of the visionary artist's revelation, the product of which is captured and concealed within his creation. It is the ever-present dynamism which underlies nature's evolutionary impetus and advantageous forms. Whether or not this explains the kangaroo turning into a spacecraft, it is difficult at this point to tell, but either way the presence of *deliberate absurdity* is present in the report.

Now, in contrast to the 'Cold War Hypothesis' is Jacques Vallée's classic ufological study, *The Passport to Magonia* (1969), which goes much further than what is classically taken to be the standard history of ufology. The most common origin, of course, is that the word 'flying saucer' was coined by Kenneth Arnold, an aviator and businessman who saw a mysterious disc over Mount Rainier, Washington in June of 1947—this, of course, further cements the Cold War hypothesis. Again, as Vallée argues, this circumscribes it into a too comfortable time period in which it can again be written off as 'experimental military technology' of the post-War years; even as a type of emergent neurosis after years of public uncertainty—a 'collective hysteria'. Kenneth Arnold's case is anecdotal, and this very anecdotal nature plagues UFO research due to its being 'merely anecdotal', in other words, a testament to its unscientific and improvable nature. In this view the phenomenon cannot, therefore, become scientifically grounded unless it can be (as it often has been) detected on radar, or, as is more difficult to prove, remnants of a crashed craft have been examined. The latter hypothesis becomes problematic, for it presupposes that the UFO phenomena is a physical, materialistic and a 'nuts-and-bolts' quantifiable 'thing'. However, from our point of view we may quite confidently attend to the 'merely anecdotal', for this, in a sense, is the best place to start when unravelling the phenomenological dimension of 'high strangeness'.

Indeed Vallée convincingly argues that rumours, anecdotes and theories relating to mysterious flying objects go as far back as 1560, contradicting many of the aforementioned theories of a more recent origin. For example, Pierre Boaistuau, author of *Histoires Prodigieuses* (*Wondrous Tales*), a sort of encyclopedia of bizarre natural phenomena and other mysteries, does an admirable job of prefiguring the history of ufology:

> The face of heaven has been so often disfigured by bearded, hairy comets, torches, flames, columns, spears, shields, dragons, duplicate moons, suns, and other similar things, that if one wanted to tell in an orderly fashion those that have happened since the birth of Jesus Christ only, and inquire about the causes of their origin, the lifetime of a single man would not be enough. (Vallée; 1975: 7)

There seems to be the persistent sense that the UFO has a desire to *cloak* itself in absurdity, almost as if its will is precisely *to confound*. Evermore complex, elaborate schemes — and a *strategic management of contexts* — seem to place the UFO firmly in the domain of dream logic. In other words, a form of deliberate entanglement and subversion of all contextual 'nets' thrown out by mankind, in his attempt to yield some coherence or meaning, are a fundamental part of its nature. And, moreover, the enormous amount of time it takes to cross-reference all accounts, as Pierre Boaistuau pointed out, would take many lifetimes.

Beginning from this perspective one might say that the 'drama' of the UFO is as persistent as it is ambiguous, and, moreover, that it is apparently a real event that has haunted man throughout the centuries under different guises. The anecdotes, fraught as they are with their unreliable translations and inevitable biases, nevertheless add to the phenomenon's mercurial nature. This, indeed, may answer for its preference for embedding its mythology on the fringes of society, thus constructing for itself a carefully protected form of mythological consciousness in man—appearing, like most mythologies, in the realm of the 'merely anecdotal', and while simultaneously being the birthplace of new stories of the eccentric, the unusual and macabre, novel and mysterious. All these stories bleed in to our collective minds, and thus they inevitably leave an indelible mark on our culture's storytelling.

We may so far summarise that the phenomenon is a collective psychological event that modifies itself over time; all the time adapting and re-modulating itself almost in an experimental nature. Our stories do the same, constantly evolving and integrating more levels of information, pushing the boundaries of the 'other' into more elaborate forms, and allowing fertile 'What ifs?' to enter the cultural consciousness. Now, whether or not its shifting nature is *our subjective doing* is as important as it is as an external phenomenon—that is, an objective 'thing'. But, until that is conclusive, we can only provide sufficient reason to penetrate its psychological and sociological 'presence'.

Here we can posit the idea of a 'psychic reality' as does Wilson in *World Famous UFOs* (2005), that is, by proposing a reality that runs 'parallel to our physical reality' and that 'ghosts, demons, poltergeists, fairies, even "vampires" are incursions from this "other reality" into our own' (2005: 186). This 'incursion' seems to make the most sense, for the phenomenon does appear to be an experimental project that keeps renewing and rewriting its methodology. Wilson continues along this line of speculation: 'Like the human race, the denizens of this other realm probably change and evolve, so their methods of drawing attention to themselves also change and evolve' (2005: 186). In a sense the phenomena can be 'read' as if it were an unfolding story, authored by someone or some 'thing'. There is also the idea that we are self-authoring the phenomena, in some deep sense, and deliberately stretching the limits of our unhealthily entrenched — or detached—views that cause a stagnation in some hidden and neglected aspect of our being.

One could even argue that mythology *itself* is a collectively sustained anecdote. Sustained, that is, by its retelling. The reason for its perseverance in our culture may highlight its importance in offering a form of sustenance to a part of our nature that is calling out in demand. Now, if there is an evolutionary imperative, an element of our collective psyches—or daemons—may partake in a cultural environment that informs the maintenance of a healthy evolution. And perhaps the language of metaphor is the most suitable vehicle for its task.

Strieber, allegedly abducted by entities related to the UFO phenomena, with his co-author, Dr Jeffrey J. Kripal, present a similar phenomenological approach by placing Strieber's experiences into a sort of 'suspension', or as the phenomenologist Edmund Husserl called it: *epoché*. Being a witness and abductee, Strieber nevertheless boldly proposes a method by which we 'discard all the gods and ghosts, the demons, the aliens, and all the stories that go with them, the heroes and their journeys and their resurrections, and re-envision our relationship with this other world objectively' (Strieber & Kripal; 2016: 44). He proposes we grapple with this newly emergent phenomenon on its *own terms*, rather than in an attempt to fit it within a ready-made mythology. What is implicit in Whitley and Kripal's approach is that we include ourselves in the unfolding narrative, assessing how our own interpretive functions distort what is understood and misunderstood, experienced or imagined.

Strieber, upon reflecting on his own experiences, perceives it as a lesson about the embodiment of our very being. In other words, perceived as a sort of cycle in which man—as he experiences his everyday existence—is subject to a series of constraints circumscribed by his very embodiment in matter. And then, released back into the timelessness at death, is reborn, re-embodied and dispersed once more. By stepping back from his experience, and when looked at it without the 'masks' of mythological projection, Whitley reflects that one is instead presented with a fundamentally metaphysical perspective concerning life and death. Says Strieber:

... we may well see that there is a cycling back and forth taking place, the movement of souls into and out of bodies, living in time and outside of time. If those of us who are descended into time can acquire an objective understanding of why we have come into this state, we can make it vastly more useful to us than it is now. (Strieber & Kripal; 2016: 244)

Phenomena as bizarre and endlessly ambiguous as the UFO or alien abduction may lead to a sort of trauma—an existential vacuum that one is only too painfully aware. To strip away all the fabrications, compensatory mechanisms—what the mystic philosopher Gurdjieff called 'buffers'—and staring into the heart of the UFO experience is, like any other phenomenological exercise, conducive to an existentially-tinted self-awareness. For Strieber, it is a case of seeing our lives as somehow reciprocal and cyclical, a matter of birth and rebirth. Interestingly, Strieber has also related that he returns to the work of Gurdjieff to recalibrate himself after these bewildering traumas. If we take Strieber's experiences as real, then it is not surprising that he should ask himself, 'Why *me?*' which, in turn, will lead to the inevitable question, 'Who am *I?*' This, I believe, is what Strieber is able to extract from his own experience of the anomalous. For, in a sense, one's own very being is as anomalous as that which it confronts—there is, in that gap of comprehension, an incursion of mystery that may cleanse habitual or 'mechanical' thinking.

In his earlier book, *Solving the Communion Enigma* (2012), Strieber emphasises the 'power of the question', being attendant to the mystery *behind* the mystery, so to speak. In doing so, he came to the conclusion that 'who we are' is 'the greatest of all mysteries'. This, of course, is the fundamental tenet of existentialism. He goes on to say that we 'present an appearance to ourselves of being a physical species that has evolved over aeons' but, he continues, this is an 'illusion that we have chosen for ourselves' and that human bodies 'are devices that we use to penetrate our attention deeply into the sensory world. But they are not us. We are something else, come here to rest ourselves and recover ourselves outside the endlessness that is our true home, and, above all, to evolve into something new' (2012: 198).

Again, we can see in Strieber's grappling with the phenomenon that there is this question of the meaning of life as well as death. Particularly he is interested in these two apparently divergent strands, for both life and death are fundament parts of evolution. The meaning occurs not when the two split away, death one way and life another, but in a sort of timeless convergence of the two—the evolutionary recognition, for Strieber, is that both life and death unify into an existential affirmation of the testing experience of life and, in Strieber's case, the extreme fringes of anomalous experience itself. We will discuss this further in the last chapter in the context of shamanism and the psychotherapy developed by Stanislav Grof.

Elsewhere Whitley makes a curious distinction regarding the 'visitors' or 'entities' in which he argues that they 'represent the most powerful of all forces acting in human culture' and that they are indeed 'managing the evolution of the human mind' or 'represent the presence of mind on another level of being' (2012:

236). He concludes that it might be mankind's fate to 'leave the physical world altogether and join them in that strange hyper-reality from which they seem to emerge' (2012: 236). Whether or not this is the destiny of an afterlife, or, a strange ascendance of mankind's mind to a higher level of experience, it is difficult to tell. And yet, implicit in these conclusions is the notion that the mind *can* know other realities, truer and more 'hyper-real' perceptions beyond that which we ordinarily experience. They urge us to seek for the *real* reality behind what is merely presented to us by our five senses.

Questions such as these are the fundamental basis of religion, esotericism and even to some extent existentialism if what informs existentialism — questions relating to human existence — is the search for the phenomenological reality that underlies the experience of the transcendental or the anomalous. If these experiences are a part of our existential reality as human beings, it is therefore within the bounds of analysis for the existentialist.

All this brings us nicely back to Colin Wilson's 'new existentialism', for Wilson incorporated Husserl's notion of the 'transcendental ego' in the fundamental recognition that there is an unconscious element with *authors*, so to speak, our experience of reality prior to our apprehension of it. It is the energy behind our ability to grasp reality at all; it is, fundamentally, the 'form-imposing' faculty. Wilson places great emphasis on Husserl's notion of 'intentionality', this active 'will' behind our perception that is 'fired' by the 'transcendental ego'. For Wilson, as it was to an extent for Husserl, insights into the transcendental ego's intentional nature would offer an insight into those states achieved in mystical visions, directing us in the direction of 'the keepers of the key to the ultimate sources of being' and to the 'unveiling of the hidden achievements of the transcendental ego' (1966: 62). Again, all this leads back to our own perceptual mechanisms, our very consciousness, and in turn this may allow us to stand back — like Strieber — and reflect more clearly on the often psychologically disorientating nature of the UFO experience.

If, for instance, something so baffles our consciousness and, in doing so, restructures our own relationship to ourselves, we may begin by reorienting our psychological mechanisms. We can see that to an extent Strieber concluded that the 'entities' themselves are managing our culture, that they are, in some deep sense, underlying mythological archetypes that run underneath our collective psyche, bursting forth occasionally into our psychic reality. One might even approach them as instrumentalities of our transcendental egos, or, for that matter, forces entirely external to us—evolutionary agents. Nevertheless, in examining our very depths we may develop a new type of logic that can integrate the intentions behind such phenomenon more generally. And, in turn, we may be our own directors, *intending ourselves in a far more active manner.*

Jorjani remarks that the 'lurid character of so many of these [alien] contacts prevents them from being taken seriously by the scientific establishment of the target society, and instead these experiences are allowed to sink into the deeper, dreamlike psychical substrate that defines the mythic folklore of a culture' (2016: 371). Whether or not this type phenomenon directly *emerges* from this 'psychical substrate' is the same question as the genesis of myth itself. Indeed, are myths 'planted', so to speak, to grow within a culture in order to shape its destiny? How are new ideas born? Such questions orientate the mind towards the study of esotericism. Strieber even refers to some of the more bizarre experiences he's encountered as 'living hieroglyphs': a mystery drama to be decoded by the interpreter. Again, there is this emphasis on *interpretation*; the hermeneutic approach as well as the phenomenological. We will return to the subject of the esoteric in more depth later on.

The fact that Strieber is a novelist, a professional storyteller, and a weaver of horror stories, is perhaps significant, for, whatever these 'entities' might be, they have certainly selected an individual with the psychological tools and skills necessary to absorb and release their (sometimes terrifying) presence into the public consciousness. As I have mentioned above, it is curious that Strieber should follow the work of Gurdjieff, whose entire mystical philosophy is underpinned by a need to jolt man out of his passivity through necessary, but sometimes painful, 'shocks'. This seems to be similar to Lachman's interpretation in that they are intended to challenge our passivity, to frustrate and reinvigorate our sense of mystery.

Now, in comparing the 'visitors' to Gurdjieff's system, Strieber remarks that, 'What I got from the visitors was friction a thousand times more potent, friction that had the power to break the soul, to plunge me into a frozen paroxysm of hatred and fear.' For, with each change in Gurdjieff's theory of octaves, there is a required 'shock' for the further evolution and development of that octave to a *higher level*. And this higher level, this higher 'I', is very much similar to what Husserl meant by the 'transcendental ego'—that which actively 'intends'. Strieber has also mentioned the fact that the whole experience might be what evolution looks and feels like when it is immediately up-close––a sudden leap, sometimes precarious, and fraught with dangers when accelerated without due caution. Similarly Wilson argues in *Introduction to the New Existentialism* (1966):

If knowledge is really to fire my *whole* being, and cause it to expand, it must not be capable of merely of exploding my childhood prejudices and releasing me into a broader world of universal knowledge; it must also enable me to understand my inner-being… In being able to stand aside from my habits of perception, I shall have discovered the secret of poetry and mysticism. (1966: 54)

Of course, Gurdjieff's philosophy is based on this notion of a 'shock' that would enable a more fully crystallized identity, a 'super-ordinate' self that enables one to 'stand aside' from habitual perception—it is with this very ability that we may understand the 'secret of poetry and mysticism'. Essentially, this is the impression one gets from Strieber's writings on the subject. They represent a disturbing but simultaneously enlightening voyage into the unconscious, inner-regions of man, in which the forces are enormous and sometimes impersonal, but nevertheless buoy up our entire being rather like a boat rests on a tumultuous and vast ocean. In other words, it is a vision into the 'life force'— that origin of all intentionality, and the energy from which the transcendental ego ignites our perceptions in our most intense states of being.

To the uninitiated these experiences might be actively detrimental, even dangerous—but with a careful phenomenological discipline, they break the shackles of our habituated consciousness and allow a far more intense experience of a reality usually blinkered from our five senses.

A Personal Note: Existentialism, UFOs and Science Fiction

Now that I have described the fundamental theories and approaches that will inform this essay, I should explain its genesis. This is important to understand my own approach to ufology.

It was sometime in 2008 when I first picked up *Alien Dawn* due to my increasing interest in the UFO phenomenon. It was, as I have mentioned, a choice based on my previous reading of Wilson's work—particularly *The Outsider*. The interest did not occur randomly or superficially; it was in part due to witnessing a UFO myself in February of that same year. At the time I was mainly interested in existentialist literature of the pessimistic variety—writers such as Michel Houellebecq and the Romanian arch-pessimist, Emil Cioran—I found particularly invigorating in the sense that it was so merciless and bold. There was something fundamentally stimulating about their firebrand approach to existence; they ranted and exploded, rather than carefully delineate their philosophies. I was, I should add, twenty-two at the time, and being in a rather working-class village probably demanded this sort of intensity merely for stimulation. My tendency at that time was to seek out existentially 'authentic' answers, and, as I was steeped in existential literature this tended to be pessimistic. It was, in short, as 'authentic' as I wanted it to be—that is, reflective of my own vacillating moods. Although I had read *The Outsider* before *Alien Dawn*, I had regarded it as an enormous acceleration of my understanding of existential literature; although strangely, I initially failed to integrate its essentially optimistic conclusion.

Seeing that *Alien Dawn* was written by the same author of this existentialist classic, I found it to be the obvious choice for a foray into the subject. I had read a lot of ufological literature before, but had found it a struggle, sometimes buying questionable titles. To the now culturally sanctioned and widely published world of existentialism and pessimistic postmodernists, ufology and other paranormal literature, by comparison, seemed kitsch and somewhat trivial. Socially and culturally, at least, it's the equivalent of sliding into the abyss. An abyss, I felt, no worse than any identified in the works of the existentialists.

And yet, strangely enough, any careful reading of the literature finds you in good company, with a wide range of impressive and intelligent writers on the subject, such as the ones mentioned above: Jacques Vallée, John E. Mack, MD and more recently, Dr Jeffrey Kripal. Despite this the whole topic is plagued by a sense of muddle-headed credulousness or fierce disbelief. Sifting through this, for witnesses, casual readers and even serious researchers, becomes a difficult task.

I was therefore left with a sense of something that was fundamentally incommunicable, and, furthermore, an incomprehensible experience to contend with. My own experience, I should add, was that merely of being a witness of a silent, apparently amorphous and changing series of lights about 30ft above our—there were three other witnesses—heads. There was the added problem of its inherent difficulty to simply describe; it was frankly *too* unusual and unlikely to convey. There is also the added problem of memory, for one can see quite easily how each witness has his own interpretation of what he saw. Nevertheless, there was a general agreement that we saw *something* fundamentally 'other'. One of the problems we all found was the fact that it was rather difficult to share with anybody else. For would there be a sympathetic listener to whom it could be described? There were a few, but more generally it was something you kept under close wrap. Also, of course, was the problem of whether it *could* be described. Finally I asked myself the question: *what does one do with the knowledge and experience of such a phenomenon?* The only answer, I found, was to read about the subject and try to understand what *meaning* it may have had for others, in an attempt to correlate as many accounts as possible and compare them with my own.

Alien Dawn took away some of the stigma of being a UFO witness, and it opened up a genuine and refreshing area fertile with novel ideas. Even though I had been stewing in a sort of materialistic pessimism for a number of years, the essentially science-fictional sensibilities underlying much of the speculation regarding the phenomena enabled a sort of inner-opening to ideas which were essentially *impersonal*. They were far more open-ended and called into question many other aspects of existence. Unlike the literature I was reading before the event, *Alien Dawn* threw up so many implications that there was a looming sense of infinity. It presented far more questions that seemed to be as genuine and in sympathy with, fundamentally, an existential frame-of-mind. The event itself represented a mystery, and understanding such mysteries allowed one to see that you were embedded in a larger mystery still. There were mysteries beyond the scope of man's own existence, and yet— knowingly or unknowingly—we were grappling with something essentially meaningful. Contrasting these ideas against each other unearthed the strangeness of being in itself, for that fundamental was no longer a consistent limitation, but part of a much larger context.

Essentially, this is what Strieber is trying to express regarding his own far more intensive experiences. He felt, like many of us, that instead of being adrift in a meaningless universe, we instead inhabit a reality with an emergent evolutionary context—a part of which our very consciousness is a significant contribution to its implicit and explicit developments.

At this point, I might add that one of the witnesses felt that the environment had become animated, and that he sensed that to some degree the woodland surrounding us was somehow conscious of the whole experience. Whether or not this was the psychological euphoria resultant of something so unusual, it is difficult to tell, but nevertheless the heightening—artificial or authentic—allowed such a sensation to occur. The experience, no doubt, was disorientating, but nevertheless it opened up a great many questions regarding our own perceptions, and each separately came to his own conclusions.

The UFO still remains a mystery, but by delving into books like *Alien Dawn*, one comes away with a myriad of other approaches, such as quantum physics, mysticism, psychology, comparative mythology, religious and esoteric ideas, even evolutionary theory. And then there's the anecdotes that temper your own, make your own absurd experience seem normal, even banal, by comparison. But what Wilson himself introduced was a steady-handed phenomenology of the phenomena. Indeed, Wilson even goes on to say in the book, '… if an important part of the purpose of these phenomena is the effect on us, then that purpose would seem to be to *decondition* us from our unquestioning acceptance of consensus reality' (1999: 326). This, it seems to me, is the essential overall effect of the UFO experience.

One of the great benefits of being introduced to the history of ufology through Wilson is that there's no shortage of further reading. A voracious reader, Wilson treads the way for any would-be researcher, providing clues and references like a Golden Thread. And even though many of his books on Atlantis and UFOs might not appear, on first glance, to be associated with his earlier work in 'The Outsider Cycle'—with its focus on the 'new existentialism'—they are on closer inspection a means to nourish and advance this phenomenological method for understanding extraordinary 'peak' states of consciousness. Through the heady final chapter of 'The Way Outside' in *Alien Dawn*, one covers most of the ground of the 'new existentialism' through to plasmas, multiple universes, holograms and even John Wheeler's *participatory anthropic principle*. Rather, it is an extension of many of the ideas presented in his earliest work, and an attempt to stretch further the analysis of unusual—and/or heightened—states of consciousness for their phenomenological value of unveiling an essential meaning.

What I felt to be one of the most insightful ideas of the book emerges when Wilson very briefly turns to the work of the science-fiction writer, Ian Watson, who wrote *The Embedding* (1973), which Wilson says, 'has claims to be one of the best science-fiction novels ever written' (1999: 350). However, it is Watson's novel *Miracle Visitors* (1978) which attempts not only to explore the mystery of UFOs, but, Wilson concludes, to 'find an answer to the mystery' (1999: 351). I would argue that Watson's work is one of the most advanced attempts at an unravelling of this entangled phenomenon that has been yet attempted, and certainly, anyone who is familiar with his work will know that he has an extraordinary and dizzying imaginative range.

Again it is significant that a novelist—like Whitley Strieber—is someone at the avant-garde when it comes to expressing something that baffles ordinary linear expression. There is a freedom that creative thinking and writing can allow, and this ought to inform many of the more analytical works in ufology. It populates the theoretical and hypothetical models with rich and novel insights. Watson had clearly studied the UFO phenomena closely and, in *Miracle Visitors*, embedded—as it were—an effective condensation of the mystery in an unfolding narrative. It is, in short, one of the most enlightening refractions from the distorted Indra's net of ufology.

As a novel it is a sort of cultural epiphenomena of the UFO phenomenon itself. The story and the ideas that inform it directly emerge out of the ufological equivalent of the collective unconscious. Indeed, it is a multilayered novel that, in compacting enormous amounts of complex narrative and hypothetical asides, reconfigures the chaos of the UFO folklore into something which, for the first time, can be seen as an evolutionary symbol—an evolutionary metaphor.

Watson himself uses similar language to describe the essential 'unknowableness' of the UFO, for in the novel he breaks this down into levels of higher and lower order 'systems' of knowledge; a sort of a hierarchy of living *episteme*:

> ... individual beings within the system cannot really know this directly. For I speak of higher-order systems of organization: of higher-order patternings. Lower-order systems cannot fully grasp the Whole of which they are the parts. Logic forbids. It is the natural principle. Which is why, when the processes of the Whole do show themselves, it is as unidentified phenomena—as intrusions into your own knowledge that can be witnessed and experienced but not rationally known: neither analysed, nor identified. Such intrusions are inestimably important. They are the goad towards higher organization. They are what urges the amoeba to evolve towards a higher life form. They are what spurs mind to evolve from natural awareness, and higher consciousness from simple mind. They are the very dynamic of the universe. (2003: 102)

French sociologist Bertrand Méheust comments in *Science Fiction and Flying Saucers* (1978) that the UFO phenomena acts like a '"super-dream" ... that works through a process of radical "absurdization"' (quoted in Kripal; 2010: 213). The 'absurdization', it could be argued, is Watson's 'unknowableness', 'experienced but not rationally known' due to their 'higher-ordering patternings'. Goading us by their absurdity—their boundary-stretching incomprehensibility—they posit the limits of human knowledge while stretching the mystery back into the heavens, that birthplace of metaphysical speculation. The very conceptual *fuzziness* of the phenomena leaves us in the dark; its informational complexity and irrationality is of course something contrary to the rationalist and mechanistic idea of a basically 'functional' i.e. unconscious universe that unpacks itself without any recourse to mystery or meaning. A universe displaced of *Why?* with *How?*—for the question of why, of course, presupposes a meaning in a cosmology of materialism that rejects meaning as merely subjective, and not present in a material world of happenstance existence.

It is worth mentioning that I am here reminded of Peter Hitchens' comments on his 'atheist period', in which he 'became an enthusiast for total rationality'. Hitchens continues by saying that he happily embraced 'the cold, sharp metric and decimal systems, disregarding the polished-in-use, apparently irrational but human and friendly measures', and this so developed that he 'sought out buildings without dark corners or any hint of faith in their shape... I longed for a world of clean, squared-off structures, places where there was no darkness' (2010: 32). Significantly this, as we will see later, may have something to do with the two hemispheres of the brain.

In this 'atheist period' the architecture, like our cosmology, offers only a *Why?* in the utilitarian sense of convenience, of materialistic practicality, or 'conservation of energy'. There is no darkness, no 'unknowableness' that draws us onward and upwards, only a sense of static values that science, even when presented as 'magic' as in one of Richard Dawkins' books, does not inspire awe, but only Eliot's 'whimper'. It is what Martha Heyneman means when she says, 'If the whole had no pattern, the part could have no meaning. It was lost in a chaos without a centre, a principle of unity, a "point"' (2001:37). Paradoxically this very 'point' is darkness itself, the parts of what we are embedded in as human beings, that remains unenlightened. This is the same darkness that represents enormous potentiality in contrast to nihilism and drifting; it is the 'deliberate unknowability' that is, in a paradoxical sort of way, directional. The cathedral, rather than the utilitarian building of the metric and measured variety, infers something more than itself; its architecture is designed in a sort of metaphorical means to cross over with the measurements of the infinite, and in doing so emerge as a visual representation of the evolutionary metaphor. *It precisely inspires because it infers more than it is*—in contrast, of course, to being merely utilitarian, inferring only its purposes of utility.

Now, in his essay, 'The Age of the World Picture', the philosopher Martin Heidegger states his belief that by 'means of this shadow the modern world extends itself out into a space withdrawn from representation... This shadow... *points to something else, which it is denied to us of today to know.'*[7] Indeed, Heidegger's shadow is what, for him, drives technological and scientific progress, for we seek out with our instruments new domains by transmuting the unknown into the *scientifically* 'known'. However, similar to Watson's posited 'unknown', this approach lends itself just as well to a mythological interpretation, for as Jordan Peterson notes: '[myth] tends to portray the generative individual consciousness eternally willing to face this unknown... in essence—in contradistinction to unconscious, impersonal, and [the] unpredictable... in light of its "seminal", active, "fructifying" nature' (1999: 181).

By delving into the field of ufology it is certain that, whether one will emerge with an evolutionary idea or not, nevertheless the task becomes the equivalent of navigating the strange world of mythological archetypes. The Jungian James Hillman has even noted that 'mythology is ancient psychology and psychology is recent mythology.' The dreamlike logic, of course, is so rich with archetypal symbolism that it seems to emerge out of a rich stream of a 'collective unconscious', and, as the UFO cloaks itself in mythical garb—or, indeed, we *capture* it in a mythologizing consciousness—it seems reasonable to suggest that one approaches it as such. Indeed, Patrick Harpur believes the most convincing 'reason for attributing mythological status to [UFO phenomena] is that, like myths, they are capable of bearing an inexhaustible number of interpretations, no single one of which can finally explain them' (2003: 123). This very interpretive nature, as we have seen, informs stories, works of fiction—all effective vehicles of the mythological imagination.

But if we venture forth into this territory it is wise to heed the words of Jordan Peterson, for it is the '"fructifying" nature of the hero's grappling with the unknown that should be the boon of his return.' It is, in other words, a call to return with something useful, practical, invigorating and fundamentally evolutionary in value. It is for this reason that I believe an active approach in the vein of Wilson's 'new existentialism' can help us converge upon the evolutionary principles that may underlie both the esoteric works of the past, and simultaneously, the emerging folklore of the UFO, offering, as it does, an evolutionary interpretation of their myriad forms and narratives that they undertake.

For, as Wilson says, if such 'psychic phenomena have a purpose it is to wake us up from our "dogmatic slumber", and galvanize us to evolve a higher form of consciousness'. Indeed, he concludes that, 'this is the only positive and unambiguous lesson we can learn from the strange mystery of the flying saucers' (1999: 186).

As we can see, from the above interpretation(s)—beginning from Heidegger's more materialistic development by positing mystery as man's primary motive force behind technological advancement—we may perceive the juxtaposition of man's orientation towards progress; scientific, spiritual and mythological. And, if anyone of these should gain undue promotion as man's primary motive, there will be resultant psychic dis-ease. It is, rather, a call for the integration of all the streams which, in their own ways, are products of a much larger evolutionary impulse and context. It is, in fact, a matter of widening our existential foundations to take the weight of a much more responsible enterprise of our future development. One could say it is a call for a catalyst as well as a buttress against the forces of an unbalanced development. In other words, it is the recognition of a psycho-social context in which we can incorporate the largest—and sometimes dangerously unrecognised—of man's impulses.

Now, we may speculate here that the UFO is a symptom and symbol of a culture on the precipice of environmental and psychic breakdown, whereby it haunts us by utilising the cultural props to appear as simultaneously a scientific phenomenon, as well as a quasi-spiritual and mythological form that defies many of the conventions of each 'conceptual net'. One might call it a dialectic in action, a gauntlet of ambiguity thrown down for minds to disentangle, or, indeed, influence a modality of thinking that might bridge the gap between man's psychic schisms. Again, as a sort of giant Zen kōan that it benefits us to understand.

Pertaining to the imaginatively expansive and therapeutic nature of symbols, PD Ouspensky notes in his essay 'The Symbolism of the Tarot' that it is 'perfectly clear that symbols are not created for expounding what are called scientific truths', and this in light of the UFO phenomena may be precisely the reason *why* it confounds science—for that might be its very intention. In fact, Ouspensky continues by saying that the 'very nature of symbols must remain elastic, vague and ambiguous, like the sayings of an oracle. Their role is to unveil mysteries, leaving the mind all its freedom' (1989: 218). By emphasising the purposeful ambiguity of 'living symbols', Ouspensky has hit upon a profoundly interesting approach towards phenomena in general, for if, like Wilson proposes, the only healthy way of approaching psychic phenomena is to heed them as wake-up calls out of our 'dogmatic slumber', then, we might grapple— on all of man's psychic levels—with a modern, living symbol that may be entirely a revolutionary paradigm unto itself. Indeed, Oswald Wirth in *Le symbolisme hermétique* says as much: 'symbols are precisely intended to awaken ideas sleeping in our consciousness. They arouse thought by means of suggestion and thus cause the truth which lies hidden in the depths of our spirit to suggest itself' (1989: 217).

Through the living symbol of the UFO, we may begin to see a semblance of unification of the mythological and the scientific/technological impulse, and through this a development of mankind may be initiated. In other words, the shadows of all our drives may be integrated—intuitive, rational, materialistic and spiritual—into an evolutionary dynamic. And as the UFO is 'withdrawn from [explicit-materialistic] representation', it nevertheless, *and as an idea*, inspires in us a speculative and intuitive approach that 'fructifies', brings new life, into areas of our psyches that may have become numb under too much materialism and 'nothing-but-ness'. Of course, such a nihilistic cosmology as presented to us in modern science may become dangerously toxic and claustrophobic, for with its closed-system approach it circumscribes man's potential to a meaningless cosmic fluke.

The UFO, then, may be a thermometer for our culture's development—and its appearance in the past may have been guiding or initiating certain other elements of our culture's unconscious drives.

It may very well be that the UFO, in its inside-out ambiguity, represents something outside of the very bounds of that which stunts man's evolutionary growth—that is, it haunts us from the periphery of the known, frustrating materialism's out-of-date boundaries by clownishly transgressing and subverting logic and the rationalist's own spiritual equivalent of the Iron Curtain.

Now, to return to Watson's *Miracle Visitors*, we may see that in his protagonist's revelation these ideas are perfectly at home in the expansive genre of science fiction:

For all *these inaccessibilities caused a fierce suction to-wards ever higher patterns of organization, towards high-er comprehension.* So molecules become long-chain mol-ecules, and these became replicating cells that transmitted information... till mind evolved, and higher mind. The universe, he realized, was an immense *simulation*: of itself, by itself. It was a registering of itself, a progressive observation of itself from ever higher points of view. (2003: 187)

Indeed, Méheust's 'super-dream' that tends towards 'absurdization'; and Jung's flying mandalas that are harbingers of a new psychic unity; and indeed Watson's 'suction' of 'inaccessibilities' towards 'ever higher patterns' do seem to be the *raison d'être* behind the UFO phenomena. This brings us to the very essence of Wilson's 'new existentialism', for its evolutionary premise enables us to unfold a phenomenological groundwork to do the integrative work on our own behalf.

In Watson, Wilson saw a genuine attempt to understand the phenomenology behind the UFO experience, and this is what lends to *Alien Dawn* a quality that is often lacking in books on ufology.

Now, before we move on to discussing esotericism and synchronicity, it is worth mentioning a story that happened between Watson and Wilson that allows us an interesting insight into the absurdity of the phenomenon. It can be taken as one pleases, as a meaningful synchronicity, or a freak accident of circumstance. But many of its elements prefigure some of the topics that we shall pursue. Watson relates:

[Wilson had] been prompted to phone me by reading my own fictional take on the UFO 'experience', *Miracle Visitors*. Colin's phone was struck by lightning through the landline either during or just after one of our conversations, causing a book fire in his room; unremarkable contacts with such as Colin Wilson seemed impossible—or maybe the lightning had something to do with the UFO phenomenon. You'd think I'd be able to remember clearly whether the lightning strike came during or after; but oh don't we mythologise ourselves?[8]

Absurdity and mythologization, as we have seen, takes a significant role in the 'drama' of the UFO phenomena. And the lightning bolt striking between the line of a researcher and a novelist, it seems, is a brilliant place to start unpacking the hermetic spirit which lies at the heart of such evolutionary metaphors...

Plasma, Signatures and the Life Force

Other than discussing Whitley Strieber's interpretations of the meaning behind his abduction experiences, I am aware that we have not directly discussed the UFO experience using any other case studies or direct, reported examples. This has been intentional, for it sets us up to explore the odd levels and layers of interpreting anomalous phenomena in general. My intention so far has been to present a general way of thinking which has close ties with esotericism. Indeed, James W. Deardorff has speculated along these same lines, for the phenomena may communicate by bypassing scientists and instead providing recipients with 'vague descriptions of extraterrestrial technological achievements that would read like magic or science fiction'. Deardorff continues:

> They might even contain a few absurdities purposely added; these... would help ensure that any scientists who happened to learn about the communications would regard them as hoaxes or fiction... Meanwhile, the message would get published, translated into various languages, and distributed throughout the world amongst other occult literature.[9]

Now, if we turn to Andrija Puharich's bizarre book, *Uri* (1974), for example, we have the same strange sense of absurdity repeated. The world-famous psychic, Uri Geller, in a moment of despair and frustration with the entities—namely one that referred to itself as 'Spectra'— condemns their 'performance' as 'stupid and idiotic', nevertheless, they perform for us, he says, 'on our level' (1974: 173–174). Performance, of course, has an important role to play in the mysteries, particularly mythological and those pertaining to esoteric schools. And although Uri *knows* of their existence, in some objective sense, he nevertheless does not know *what they mean*; that is, precisely what existential value that this holds for him, or indeed, for anyone else. In fact, Uri Geller, despite his flamboyant reputation, is like the rest of us when facing this mystery. And although he has had, according to his own account and Puharich's, direct experience, he is nevertheless rational and sober-minded as one can be about such a challenging experience. Condemning it as such a stupid performance, in fact, is a fairly rational approach, and is not suggestive of someone who wants to pull the wool over anyone's eyes concerning something so apparently miraculous.

Uri asks the crucial question of, 'What is it *doing* to us?' His answer, as we have seen, is an exasperated shrug. They perform for us 'on our level' is his basic insight, and our level, fundamentally, cannot go beyond itself.

Despite this, Puharich is provided with a series of unusual explanations of the functions of the soul:

I was given a new concept which was to imagine that all souls are like a vase (i.e., a physical pot). Each vase-soul exists in a rotational, gravitational field. When one perturbs the vase-soul, wavelets go out into the universe field. It is very much like dropping a pebble in water—wavelets will radiate outward. The perturbation of the vase-soul in the rotational gravitational field is experience. (1974 :195)

Again, this strikes anyone familiar with esoteric literature as strikingly consistent with many occult doctrines, particularly theosophy or something uttered by Alice Bailey. The language even reminds us more of David Bohm's 'implicate order' and quantum theory which has, over recent years, become increasingly embedded in New Age literature for its variety of versatile models and metaphors. What is more striking is that Puharich does not pursue the notion that the 'vase-soul' is, in some sense, a description of the UFO itself. The UFO, of course, often has a vase-like appearance and its effects, which are experienced or witnessed, are duly influential in their 'perturbation' of everyday existence.

There is the sense that the soul—or the UFO—is a 'spill over' into matter which, as the soul is embodied, is subject to the limitations of time and space. This is also evocative of Lurianic Kabbalah developed by Isaac Luria (1534–1572), for which his concept of *tzimtzum* is a sort of 'concealment' or 'contraction' of God. Gary Lachman, in *The Caretakers of the Cosmos* (2013), describes the process of *tzimtzum*:

> Once the *tzimtzum* created the void, Adam Kadmon, the Primordial Man, appeared... Out of the eyes, nose, mouth and ears of Adam Kadmon come flashing lights, emanations of the divine creative energies. These form the *sephiroth*, or vessels, designed to contain these energies... (2003: 32)

The human being, in Kabbalah, is an expression of these energies that are contained and simultaneously shed forth into the material existence. We, as expressions of this cosmic schism, are responsible for a type of repair work which Luria called *tikkun*, which Lachman describes as a restoration 'of the shattered *sephiroth*' and that our job is to 'heal the rift between the opposites, and unify the polarized masculine and feminine aspects of God' (2003: 34). Again, the similarity to Puharich's alleged extraterrestrial contact with Spectra leaves us with the distinct sense of esoteric knowledge being encoded within the anomalous experience. What left Uri feeling frustrated and bewildered left Puharich contending with the mysteries of human existence—there is the sense, in the UFO experience, of a deliberate friction being used to erode consensual reality, and within these fractures of reality they smuggle in new concepts for the understanding of our existential position. They present, in a peculiar way, a new cosmological and ontological model.

The engineer Bryant Reeve wrote a book with the significant

title of *The Advent of the Cosmic Viewpoint* (1965), in which he proposes a similar hypothesis to the one presented in this essay. Indeed, Reeve began from a wish to understand the physical nature of the UFO (being an engineer with a distinctly scientific orientation) but instead found that only philosophy and metaphysics could do justice to any comprehensive understanding. Reeve, after considering the evidence substantially, concluded that it demanded a radical cosmological reorientation, and that it was essentially a psycho-spiritual or esoteric 'event' of enormous significance.

There is, in all this, something that hints towards what William James described as a vast 'continuum of cosmic consciousness, against which our individuality builds but accidental fences, and into which our minds plunge as into a mother-sea or reservoir'. Again, this relates to both consciousness and the 'vase'/'vessel' imagery used in Puharich's 'contact' and Kabbalistic cosmology. It is significant, then, that in each approach the human being is considered deeply involved in the universe, and whose position is in direct contrast to the sense of contingency and meaninglessness implicit in a strictly materialistic cosmos. Also, as we have seen in the case of Strieber, there was a sense that the phenomenon was attempting to subvert our ordinary understanding of life and death.

Here it is worth returning to the 'new existentialism' to elucidate what might be called the 'cosmic viewpoint', for Wilson states in *Religion and The Rebel* (1957) this way of seeing may:

... easily be called religion. It is a way of thought which, like the religious way, regards man as *involved* in the universe, not just a spectator and observer, a sort of naturalist looking at the universe through a magnifying-glass and murmuring: 'Mmm. Most interesting.' Existentialism states that *the most important fact about man is his ability to change himself.* (1990: 148)

In short, it is by changing our perception of ourselves, and recognising that we are an *active* component in a meaningful cosmos, that we begin to actualise our far-reaching potentialities. This is a much more invigorating way of living in the world, and in doing so activates the deeper reserves of the 'life force' to meet the challenges that we face in the real world. Furthermore, implicit in the recognition of a 'cosmic viewpoint' is an evolutionary context, or directive, which further converges with our revitalised momentum, our active *engagement* with the direction that the life force directs itself—that is, towards Ian Watson's 'higher-organization', the 'very dynamic of the universe'.

By recognising this meaningful nature of the cosmos, there is also another element that allows us to 'read into' the meanings contained there within: that is, the universe becomes interpretable through a hermeneutic phenomenology. The 'flame of consciousness' is able to bring forward the symbols and language of what Jacob Boehme called the 'signatures', which Wilson—again in *Religion and The Rebel*—describes: 'just as an expert can find a criminal's fingerprint on every object from a glass vase to a human throat' (1990: 158). It is, Wilson continues, the ultimate mysticism of the West, providing a scientific insight into the mechanisms of the universe, as well as providing a simultaneous glimpse into William Blake's visions of the infinite in a grain of sand. Wilson sees that the '"Life Force" has its own deep inscrutable aims and methods in this world of physical reality', and this is precisely what the mystic can detect in those states of intense visionary consciousness.

This active approach to consciousness is indeed to what Jacques Vallée dedicated his classic book in ufology, *Passport to Magonia* (1969). He summarises it precisely:

... for the few who have gone through all this and have graduated to a higher, clearer level of perception of the total meaning of that tenuous dream that underlies... human history, for those who have recognised, within themselves and in others, the delicate levers of imagination and will not be afraid to experiment with them. (1975: 154)

In evoking the transformational power of art, Vallée continues to say, that like 'Picasso and his art, the great UFO Master shapes our culture, but most of us remain unaware of it' (1975: 160). Layers, like the varieties of applied paint on a canvas, bring forth something once implicit, something hovering in the mind's eye of the artist. Wherever these visions or ideas come from is, in a sense, as mysterious as the arrival of any anomalous event. The imagination in art, of course, becomes a transit for the life force, providing as it does a vast enough medium for its expression. Rather like Boehme's signatures, Vallée's expression of a 'clearer level of perception' that enables a vision into the 'dream that underlies history' is an imaginative leap into the evolutionary drives underlying existence itself. And as far as we know, human beings are the life force's most advanced expression.

This artistic vision was also experienced by another science-fiction writer, Philip K. Dick, whose many books have deeply impacted modern Hollywood with films like *Total Recall*, *Blade Runner* and *Minority Report*, among many others—directly or indirectly—attributed to his name. His novels often invoke what he called the 'pluriform' nature of our universe; its many layers and levels of alternate timelines (often dystopic in nature); varieties and shades of realities that exist alongside our 'ordinary' world of lived experience. In 1974 Dick claims to have undergone an unusual experience rather evocative, particularly in its use of language, of Puharich's and Luria's 'energies', or Boehme's 'signatures'. I quote from his visionary 1977 essay, 'If You Find This World Bad, You Should See Some of the Others':

[the vision] resembled plasmic energy. It had colors. It

moved fast, collecting and dispersing. But what it *was*, what he was—I am not sure even now, except I can tell you that *he had simulated normal objects and their processes so as to copy them and in such an artful way as to make himself invisible within them... By this I mean that during that short period—a matter of hours or perhaps a day—I was aware of nothing that was not the Programmer.* All the things in our pluriform world were segments or subsections of him. Some were at rest but many moved, and did so like portions of a breathing organism that inhaled, exhaled, grew, changed, evolved toward some final state that by its absolute wisdom it had chosen for itself. *I mean to say, I experienced it as self-creating, dependent on nothing outside it because very simply there was nothing outside it* [my italics]. (Quoted in Dick; 1996: 251–252.)

In this phenomenologically rich description of what is evidently a very striking event—Dick went on to write a gargantuan *Exegesis* that endlessly meditated on what he had undergone—we can see a series of correspondences with what we have pursued in this essay so far. Firstly, there is the artistry and embedded nature of its presence, that is, it is—to use Dick's phraseology—'pluriform', but also somehow disguised, not in, but *as* the environment itself. He refers to it in the language of phenomenology as 'the Programmer', which is immediately reminiscent of Husserl's 'transcendental ego'—that Will which underlies our perceptions; the origin of the intention behind the intentionality, so to speak. Dick refers to it as 'self-creating' and 'dependent on nothing outside', for it simply *is*—a self-contained, evolving conglomerate of energy. There is also something inside out about the whole experience, for at first Dick describes it as a plasmic energy, contracting into a point and then dispersing, presumably, into *the environment itself.*

In a novel that attempted to dramatically portray and grapple with this anomaly, Dick labelled it by the acronym VALIS, which is short for: Vast Active Living Intelligence System. And in keeping with our esoteric trajectory, Dick indeed called one of his essays in his famed *Exegesis* with the tongue-in-cheek and Madame Blavatsky-esque title of 'The Ultra Hidden (Cryptic) Doctrine: The Secret Meaning of the Great System of Theosophy of the World, Openly Revealed for the First Time'. (Humour, it could be argued, was the one thing that prevented Dick from becoming something like a megalomaniac guru, or, indeed a cult-like figure like L. Ron Hubbard who established the Church of Scientology.)

In his remarkable segments of *Exegesis*, Dick propounded his extraordinary grip of a transcendental form of phenomenology, seeing as it were 'signatures' in our very cosmic and psychological constitution. Furthermore, like the Kabbalah he believed that what was demanded was a sort of 'self-repair'. Indeed, he continues by saying that this includes *rebuilding our world* (which he calls 'sub-circuit' in this complex reflection):

> via linear *and* orthogonal time changes (sequences of events), as well as continual signaling to us both en masse and individually (*to us received subliminally by the right brain hemisphere, which gestalts the constituents of the messages into meaningful entities*), *to stimulate blocked neural (memory) banks within us to fire and hence retrieve what is there* [my italics]. (1996: 327)

As imaginative and inventive as Dick was, it is curious that such an anomalous experience—which, in its odd form of 'plasmic' energy resembles the UFO phenomena—led to an expounding on metaphysical, even religious terms. There is a sense that it 'reprogrammed' him; indeed, he even says he saw *by* its light—he saw everything as permeated by 'the Programmer' (or the transcendental ego). Yet, he goes further by postulating a physical as well as cosmological theory that includes *us* in the remembrance—Plato's Anamnesis—of things not only past, but of our role in the cosmos itself. It is worth comparing Dick's conclusion to Wilson's in *Access to Inner Worlds* (1983), in which Wilson emphasises that it is *'we* who transform... the raw material of perception into what we see. Perception is a sculpture, a moulder of reality... I fire it like an arrow' (quoted in Stanley; 2016: 54). Wilson concludes by saying that the 'world is a delightful place, full of hidden meanings'. We can see that Dick used similar language, positing us to 'fire and hence retrieve what is there', but, significantly, this reconstitution of a more meaningful reality is received—or added to our perceptions—by our *right brain*, which, as Dick points out *'gestalts the constituents of the messages into meaningful entities'*. In other words, it brings the 'bits' of reality into a unified and fundamentally *meaningful* whole.

Like the artist, the right brain's repair work takes fragmentary, essentially chaotic mixtures of paint, rock, marble and sound, and from them it sculpts, moulds and presents something that is strikingly meaningful—something implicit and organised. In a sense our very consciousness, by partaking in the universe itself, is 'repairing' precisely by its bringing forth a new order of meaning into an essentially 'damaged' cosmos of forms struggling to become more than the sum of their parts.

To frame this argument in a larger context, we will return to the 'new existentialism' to explore the fundamental cosmological principles that affirm the enormous importance of consciousness, and the imagination, in the *actualisation* of the evolutionary metaphors.

The Cosmology of Deep Intentionality

An intrinsic part of Wilson's 'new existentialism' is a cosmology, or what he called a 'basic metaphysic', which in its earliest form emerges in the chapter 'World Without Values' in *The Outsider*. For it is in this chapter that Wilson formulates the 'background of values' in which the power of our will—in its most active sense— can be most effectively exercised. His simple formulation runs thus: 'No motive, no willing.' However, by stating that 'motive is a matter of *belief*' Wilson underlines the importance of having something *a priori believed* in order to provide the motivation with a sufficient degree of will. Indeed, if belief lacked completely the individual would find motivation for doing anything at all impossible, leading to a complete negation of freedom. Wilson continues by saying 'belief must be the belief in the *existence* of something; that is to say, it concerns what is *real*. So ultimately, freedom depends upon the real' (1978: 49).

From this statement—that freedom depends upon the real— we then have to pursue the question: What is *real*? For most of us this question remains vague and difficult to articulate. Certainly, it is not an easy question to answer and has troubled philosophers for millennia. The idea of the *real* underlies epistemology—the investigation and theory of *what can be known*—and ontology; or that which underlies our very knowledge and experience of our *being*.

These are not abstract concepts dreamt up by philosophers alienated from both the world and themselves. In fact, these two concepts constitute what we recognise as significant elements of human consciousness in relation to other forms of consciousness. For example, PD Ouspensky understood consciousness not as a thing in itself, but a description of a state in which we become aware of one or more of our psyche's functions. These ideas are, in a sense, historical developments within the domain of human consciousness, reflected in our cosmological development, and thus determine the psychological ambience in which man finds himself and his culture.

In fact, as EF Schumacher points out, man is 'capable of being conscious of [his own] consciousness; not merely a thinker, but a thinker capable of watching and studying his own thinking' (1978: 26). Furthermore, he identifies human consciousness as 'recoiling upon itself' and thus opening up 'unlimited possibilities of purposeful leaning, investigating, exploring, formulating and accumulating knowledge' (26). Of course, this uniquely human trait has equally enormous advantages and disadvantages, for as man knows more about the universe he can witness his stature decrease with his realisations—and yet, as we have seen, this can also work in the opposite direction by providing us with an evolutionary and optimistic impetus for motivation and development of a healthy will.

In both *Beyond the Outsider* (1965) and *Super Consciousness* (2009)—two books that span Wilson's work from near beginning to end—Wilson outlines the history of philosophy to present 'a basis for a new existentialism.' For Wilson, the fundamental problem of the human situation is 'the problem of the clash between man's inner world and the alien world "out there"' (1985: 85–86). Effectively he begins from this foundation of *context*—the 'background of values', or, one could say a cosmological framework that relates to man and man to the cosmos. From this point he argues that the Greek philosophers proceeded beyond this problem by simply rejecting the physical world. Therefore, for some Greek thinkers such as Socrates or Plato, only the world of ideas remained as the *ultimate* reality. Of course, this is reflected in Plato's notion of the Forms, those immortal and perfect 'ideas' which lie outside of space and time. The split between spirit (or mind) and matter was clearly defined in Greek thought, and so much so that Socrates faced his death stoically believing that the spirit, in essence, is all that really matters. His mortal shell of mere matter, of course, would be shed and he'd be free to explore—in non-corporeal form—the world of spirit; the true home of the philosopher.

Whereas Plato believed that 'ideas are the pathway to the infinite', it was Aristotle who pursued and initiated the scientific method as we know it today. Aristotle unlike Plato focused upon the natural and material world and began to collect and correlate observable facts. Raphael's 16th century painting *The School of Athens* in fact depicts Plato as pointing up towards the heavens while Aristotle, holding his hand horizontally—as well as his copy of *Nicomachean Ethics* under his other arm—in contrast to Plato's 'vertical' world of ideas in which Plato represents the opposite of Aristotle's either/or, logic-bound and matter-of-fact approach. In essence, Plato's is more metaphysical in the sense that it proposes something *a priori* to everything else, a perfected world beyond the world of matter. Yet, even Socrates is the beginning of this 'break' from an even more spiritual tradition, and as one commentator has noted, the pre-Socratics were much more orientated towards an intimation and 'intuition of the world in its entirety' whereas post-Socratic philosophy 'surrendered to logic, in the belief that everything could be apprehended and explained with the help of this new instrument' (1993: 17).

In *Super Consciousness: The Quest for the Peak Experience* (2009), Wilson says that it was 'Aristotle rather than Plato who exercised the greatest influence on the development of the Western mind' (2009: 134). Indeed, he goes on to point out that the development of the great religions of Hinduism, Buddhism, Christianity, Judaism and Islam were of 'immense importance for the development of human culture' for these provided a 'backdrop of values' in which civilizations and individuals were able to function in a meaningful universe, a development that was crucial for the development of human consciousness at that point in time. Wilson continues by pointing out the importance of St Augustine's objection to science 'on the grounds that it prevented man from focusing upon the most important thing of all—his relation to God.' Gods, and higher intelligences for the people of the past, provided an ample amount of motive force to bolster the willpower behind the development of civilization. Moreover, it provided an *impersonal* goal that transcended the sense of contingency that would have been extremely dangerous for the evolution of man's consciousness in those early stages.

Before further summarising Wilson's overview of the history of philosophy, it is worth returning to the cosmological—as well as metaphysical—ideas that begin to emerge in our examination of the new existentialism. In *The Breathing Cathedral* Martha Heyneman says that, 'Today, we see rising before us a new shape. We can see its dim outlines through the fog... but we haven't yet come ashore. We don't yet *inhabit* our new picture of the universe' (2001: 18). Now, each of us in childhood similarly *inhabits* a cosmology that seems to us safe and basically well-meaning, yet as we grow older uncertainty sets in and we begin to feel uncertain about *what can be known* as well as uncertain about *who we truly are*. Again, this is an epistemological as well as an ontological realisation—a fundamental existential awakening that may be life-changing for some. Indeed, Wilson discusses in his essay 'Science—And Nihilism' his own breaching of his 'cosmological comfort-zone' when he was reading Einstein at about the age of ten. He says that he was suddenly 'struck by a terrible thought' when he thought about motion as being 'relative' for he suddenly saw how 'parochial' our earth-bound view is in the cosmic perspective. Quite ironically Wilson had been studying science because it gave him:

> ... a comforting sense of incontrovertible fact, of some universal truth, bigger than our trivial human emotions and petty objectives... But now Einstein was telling me that I could find no certainty in science. I was like a devout Christian who has suddenly been convinced there is no God. *I felt as if I had*

been standing apparently on solid ground, and it had suddenly opened up beneath my feet [my italics]. (1998: 46–47)

This brings us back around to the idea of *the real*—that 'solid ground'—being the motivating force behind the *will*. As a result of this realisation Wilson fell into a state of despair and despondency. It was enormously difficult for him to fight off the futility *of all endeavours*, intellectual or otherwise, after this frightening realisation of the unknowable void. There suddenly seemed an *impossibility of knowledge*, and as a result, an *impossibility of being* in its wake—for how can one go on living, at least satisfactorily, after such an earth-shattering realisation of our own universal insignificance?

Effectively it is this problem that the whole Outsider Cycle was pitted against, for it is the fundamental question of the Absolute Yes versus the Absolute No. The Romantics, as they are studied in *The Outsider*, certainly show many instances when they are able to feel sensations—intellectually as well as emotionally—that gave assent to a sense of universal optimism. And yet they were unable to *pin it down*—the next day each vision would be difficult to articulate, to *be known*, in the fullest sense of the word. Certainly, the vision, which may have been authentic and real, begins to recede, taking upon it a cadence of bitter and ironic unreality.

Certainly, they could capture these visions in powerfully evocative poems and vivid landscapes infused with vitality and ecstatic yea-saying, but so few of them were able to construct a philosophy strong enough to hold back the tumultuous currents of suicidal despair. The sense of 'unreality' returned with an overwhelming fullness of force. Wilson writes, 'The Romantics... believed that the "moments of vision" cannot be controlled. Pushkin compared the poet's heart to a coal which glows red when the wind of inspiration blows. But he cannot *make* it blow; he just has to sit and wait' (2009: 9). It is this fundamentally passive and defeatist tone that underlies many of the romantics, and again, Wilson attempted to show an active methodology by which we could fully comprehend and integrate this fundamental sense of a greater reality, and allow the coal of the heart to once again glow with flame—but this time, by an act of motive force based on something existentially *substantial* and *real*.

In his introduction to *Mysteries* (1978) he also notes that there is something 'fundamentally queer about the universe' and that it 'contradicts our assumption that there are no questions without answers' and, most disturbingly, our very minds seem somewhat unsuited for thinking about these problems. This leads to many philosophers taking the position that human existence is basically a short, brutal accident that evolved a painful form of self-consciousness. For some philosophers and writers, such as the horror writer HP Lovecraft, the Romanian arch-pessimist Emil Cioran, to the contemporary British philosopher, John Gray, consciousness itself is a mournful agony that is better off not existing at all. Indeed, the latter seems to prefer the 'silence of animals': animals whose consciousness has not yet come to grips with time and what it infers—an end to its own being: death and universal contingency. Our sense of motive, in the face of a pessimistic view of reality, recedes proportionally.

A death-haunted mankind aware of his own demise in a meaningless cosmos results in the belief that the cosmos had best have remained *uninhabited by mind*. That is, the awareness of non-meaning is the most ironic development of all. From this point of view, their visions of an all-seeing, all-knowing God—in whatever shape or form—are perceived as a sadomasochist and should be disowned. None of them, apparently, seemed to see this as a type of projection implicit in their own philosophical conclusions. *This*, essentially, is what Wilson challenged in his Outsider Cycle.

Nevertheless, a cosmology ejected of all meaningful contexts and purpose is still a cosmology. That is, even if it is a *chaos* rather than a cosmos (cosmos is the Greek word for an orderly universe rather than a chaotic one). And in any cosmology, as Heyneman points out, our knowledge and imagination are entirely 'contained, consciously or unconsciously, within it' and, furthermore if '... the vessel is shattered and the image has no shape, impressions have no meaning.' She continues:

> We have no stomach for them—no place inside ourselves to keep them. We are immersed in them, they flow over our surfaces in a ceaseless stream, but *we are unable to extract any nourishment from them to add to the structure and the substance of an understanding of our own upon which we might base a coherent and deliberate life.* (2001: 6)

Again, we are back to Wilson's original formulation that motivation—through *belief* or a cosmology—is *a priori* crucial for a healthy will. Once this has been shattered, one falls into a lower state of vitality, even despair, without any real reason to *will* anything at all. So, in effect, our beliefs and our cosmologies are fundamentally one and the same, *for they are interior models of the universe.* Now, what is *real* is not necessarily what is 'out there', but also 'in here'; that is, within our deeper layers of consciousness. Indeed, it is reminiscent of what the Indian mystic, Nisargadatta Maharaj, meant when he said, 'The real does not die, the unreal never lived.' The 'real', in short, is also an act of becoming into being; it is a motive force that wills itself into existence.

Now this is the point where we can return to Wilson's outline of philosophy and, more importantly for this essay, return to the UFO phenomenon. For the real question is: *into what philosophical context do UFOs emerge into our human story?* This is the same approach as descriptive phenomenology, for it attempts to understand the *psychological reality* of the UFO phenomena rather than the technological or physical reality. This is fundamentally the contradistinction between two modes of philosophic thought which Wilson identifies as the 'two pockets in the billiard table of philosophy: materialism and idealism' (2009: 178). What we might ask is how the UFO emerges from—or into—a collective philosophical zeitgeist, and if this is so, *what does it signify philosophically as well as phenomenologically?*

Jacques Vallée identified this problem in his book *The Invisible College* (1975), where he states that the UFO 'constitutes *both* a physical entity with mass, inertia, volume etc., which we can measure, *and* a window toward another mode of reality' (2014: 4). Vallée continues, 'These forms of life may be similar to projections; they may be real, yet a product of our dreams. Like our dreams, we can look into their hidden meaning, or we can ignore them. But like our dreams, they may also shape what we think of as our lives in ways that we do not yet understand' (2014: 4). This 'hidden meaning' is the occulted aspect of the UFO phenomenon, for it is this element that is most readily *interpreted*, and offers a unique insight into our philosophical categories and phenomenological attendance to a phenomenon so intrinsically linked with the unconscious mechanisms, of both the individual and society at large.

At this point it is worth returning to the genre of fiction that best navigates these 'in-between' territories—science fiction.

Stan Gooch in his essay 'Science Fiction as Religion'[10] provides an important idea which will help elucidate just why the genre of science fiction can provide glimpses into new and emergent metaphysics. For, where science fails—in providing meanings and speculations in the 'large picture' of human values—science fiction steps in and provides a 'surrogate belief system' and most of the modern cults—from such as Scientology to the Aetherius Society—have as their psychological aim a unification of 'science and religion'. In Gooch's words, 'modern religion and science fiction, therewith seem to be struggling towards a common meeting point—though they have as yet not reached it.' Science fiction realises that science cannot provide emotion and experience and, in doing so, compensates by trying to 'infuse those elements into scientific frameworks or cosmologies', also, of course, science cannot allow itself to wonder, so again science fiction makes up for this lack.

In his 2016 novel *The Thing Itself*, Adam Roberts has his protagonist say—in truly Kantian fashion—that our 'universe is being determined by the thing itself, and by say—the consciousness of the sentient beings perceiving the thing itself.' The 'thing itself', of course, is Immanuel Kant's notion of the *noumenon*, that which cannot be known outside of the limits of our perceptual 'categories'. To return to *Beyond the Outsider*, Wilson describes Kant's basic philosophy as being concerned with how the mind creates the universe *as we perceive it*. He continues to say that true, 'there is an unknowable reality "out there"—the *noumena*, but it is unknowable precisely because it does not need to obey our laws, and so cannot enter our perceptions, or even our reason' (1965: 91). Nevertheless, Wilson argues, it was the philosopher Johann Gottlieb Fichte who went beyond this problem and asked the crucial question of: 'Can I "create" the universe, and yet not be aware that I am doing so?' (1965: 91).

Proceeding from this question, Adam Roberts presents the problem with a great deal of clarification. Upon reflecting on the mysterious 'thing itself', or noumenon, his character concludes that the 'thing is vital, not inert' and that the 'twenty-first century atheists peer carefully at the world around them and claim to see no evidence for God, when *what they're really peering at is the architecture of their own perceptions*' [my italics]. Indeed, what they see, Roberts writes, is simply the 'Spars and ribs and wire-skeletons—there's no God there…' but, he asks with great insight, '… strip away the wire-skeleton, and think of the cosmos without space or time or cause and substance, and ask yourself: is it an inert quantity?' (2016: 326–327).

Now, what is evidenced in Roberts' novel is an attempt to unify and explore the limits of science fiction and religious belief through the philosophic framework of Kant's metaphysics. Through the 'architecture of their own perceptions' man perceives in his universe, and in himself, the limits of his own closed-system of values. Yet, what is implicit in this realisation is what Wilson calls a 'tri-alism'; that is, an addition to our usual understanding of Cartesian dualism—mind/body, spirit/matter, and so on. Instead, what is implicit in this understanding is that, as well as a 'contemplating mind ("I think") looking out at alien nature', there are two I's; 'one is the "I think", and the other the "transcendental ego".' Of course, this relates directly to Descartes' famous edict that *Cogito ergo sum* (I think, therefore I am). What Fichte and Wilson are really pointing out is that, behind the scenes of our usual perceptions, there is an 'invisible' 'I' which manifests the 'texture', as it were, and meanings that appear to underlie our apprehension of reality. And instead of 'looking out at the universe from its armchair' we need now to recognise that there are two I's, 'two faces, one to look out, one to look inward towards the "hidden I", the transcendental ego'. It would not be a stretch to say that the transcendental ego is our most esoteric dimension; for how it works, of course, requires a complex array of language and concepts to untie its mysterious involvement in our perceptions.

In an amended Epilogue to *The New Existentialism* (1966), Wilson provides some insights into what he calls his 'basic metaphysic', and this offers a valuable insight that may further our investigation into anomalous phenomena. As the UFO, according to Vallée, operates on the divide between dream and our 'here and now' reality—between our psychological and the material worlds—the transcendental ego too, in some odd way, may operate at a deeper level than we ordinarily understand. Indeed, one could say that the transcendental ego is a sort of 'reality structurer'. Now by forwarding a basic 'doctrine of the will' that aims to uncover the 'unconscious layers of will and intention, *of which you were previously not aware'*, it is significant that Wilson points out that *the deeper layers of our intentionality awaken in mystical experiences.* For in these experiences we lose our general sense of alienation—moreover, an alienation that is 'due to lack of contact with one's intentional layers'. Referring to this as our 'deep intentionality' what Wilson is really presenting here is his 'basic metaphysic'—or cosmology—that enables us, like Roberts' protagonist, to see the universe *not* as an inert quantity, but instead as an *active quality—constituting as well as sculpted by—the transcendental ego.*

Philip K. Dick may have envisioned this when he posed the 'Zebra' hypothesis which posits the idea of a God that disguises himself as the environment. Similarly, in his essay 'If You Find This World Bad, You Should See Some of the Others' he asks a similar question: if God 'wears' our universe like so many garments in a wardrobe, how do we know when this universe is being worn by this overtly style-conscious God? Now, it is not difficult to switch this idea around and say: what inhabits our universe is our 'deep intentionality' which, through us, 'wears' our perceptions of our world without us being aware of its presence. This is basically Fichte's challenge to Kant's notion of the noumenon. In fact, the transcendental ego is the part of us that bounds our consciousness of the thing itself. It does so by providing a 'livable reality' rather than an overwhelming influx of information—in short, it blinkers us in interest of our own practical survival. Man, bound by the phenomenal world, therefore has no direct access to the metaphysical realities that lie behind his categories—his structures and frameworks of perception—that en-frames human consciousness. That is, unless the intentional energies are fired up enough to access these deeper realms of the psyche, these deeper levels of intentionality.

Similarly to Philip K. Dick's 'Zebra' and Adam Roberts'

'active noumenon', Madame Blavatsky in her enormous book, *The Secret Doctrine* (1888), states that the 'noumenon can become a phenomenon on any plane of existence only by manifesting on that plane through an appropriate basis or vehicle' (2012: 20). Now, whether the UFO manifests as an aspect of the noumenon becoming phenomenon, it is almost impossible to say. But, if we begin to understand the phenomenon on its own bizarre terms, we can see how it effectively subverts our ordinary categories and challenges our Aristotelian either/or sensibilities by posing a both/and anomalous 'event'.

Here one may turn to Carl Jung's curious dream of October 1958—briefly discussed in his autobiography *Memories, Dreams, Reflections* (1962)—in which he saw 'lens-shaped metallic gleaming disks', which he identified as two typical UFOs that proceeded to fly directly towards him as he was standing alongside his lake in Bollingen. As they briefly hovered about his person they quickly flew off, leaving him alone for a short period until another UFO appeared; again this was lens-like but this time it had an extension of a sort of 'magic lantern'. As it was directing its attention towards him he suddenly awoke with the lingering thought that, 'We always think that U.F.O.s are projections of ours. *Now it turns out that we are their projections. I am projected by the magic lantern as CG Jung. But who manipulates the apparatus?'* [my italics] (1995: 355). Perhaps it was the transcendental ego, that deep intentional part of our being that showed itself to Jung in a symbolic dream?

Phenomenologically Jung's dream leaves us with much to think about. For Jung is essentially passive in this dream; indeed, he is *projected by the UFO itself.* His very existence is bestowed by these lens-like disks, equipped as they are with a sort of projection unit in the form of a magic lantern. Like Blavatsky's noumenon becoming the phenomenon, Jung is projected by the unknown incursion of anomalous flying 'observers', as it were. Now, as this was Jung's dream we can ask the inside-out question—which relates well to dream logic—by seeing if Jung's own 'dream identity'—his self as experienced in the dream—is indeed a product of an aspect of his higher-self. In other words, one might ask what aspect of Jung projected the dream in the first place?

The new existentialism lays important emphasis on the essential hierarchical nature of consciousness; lower levels of consciousness become increasingly diffuse, disintegrated, whereas higher forms of consciousness—such as the mystical experience or the 'peak experience'—become synthesised and integrated into the greater whole of our being.

At this point it will benefit us to step back and once again ask the fundamental existential questions. Indeed, questions such as: Who am I? What is the meaning of existence? become impossible to answer in our ordinary states of consciousness because, in some sense, they are at the very substratum of our being. In other words, these questions are in a sense already answered for at a level *below the iceberg* of ordinary consciousness; they are what propel us into being in the first place—and the very reason for *something rather than nothing at all*. This 'deep intentionality' is effectively the Life Force.

Now, as we increase our consciousness we also *include* these deeper layers into our being; we integrate ourselves more fully and these answers become more self-evident. In fact, we might lose our general sense of alienation altogether—this, of course, being the fundamental insight of the mystical experience, or *gnosis* (meaning knowledge): all is one; our being and the universe are ultimately *knowable* and, moreover, inseparable. 'When you awake,' writes Wilson, 'your top layers come to life first; i.e. are suffused with conscious energy, like blood flowing in the veins' but when these deeper layers of you also integrate into your 'top layers' of ordinary consciousness, there comes bubbling up the 'deep intentionality' which is, for all intents and purposes, the 'reality structurer' as well as a source of our vital energies (1995).

Indeed, as we are not normally aware of these profound resources of energy they—rather like Jung's dream UFO— effectively project our very being; they are, as it were, the foundational dynamism that maintains and energises our 'architectures of perception'. Just as Roberts points out the 'dynamic' quality of Kant's noumenon, so it is with Jung's two-way projecting UFO; both, in a sense, are representative of the deeper levels of consciousness—that level of what Wilson calls 'deep intentionality'. It is this realisation implicit in the 'new existentialism' that constitutes Wilson's essential cosmology, and furthermore it helps us illuminate the perceptual and consciousness-changing experiences associated with the UFO phenomenon more generally.

To extend these insights further it is worth turning again to the work of Carl Jung whose 'active imagination' and 'enantiodromia' may provide us with further insights into the nature of anomalous phenomena. Firstly, the basic definition of the enantiodromia is the tendency for things to turn into their opposites; a sort of governing principle that ensures a general balance of opposites. And yet, to see the UFO phenomena merely as a sort of psychic compensatory mechanism is too reductive—but, in spite of that, its very actions—its theatrical and absurdist performance—may be an *initiation* of sorts. That is, representative of a challenge that is to be overcome—a kōan designed to integrate a deeper understanding into the nature of reality, and particularly consciousness' role in the making of that reality.

If such phenomenon emerges out of a sort of deep wellspring of intentionality, that is *not* to say they are mere compensatory mechanisms acting on a sort of 'automatic-response' level. In other words, they are not the equivalent of an unconscious 'reflex-arc' that merely reacts to external conditions without any will of their own. In fact, there is the difficult realisation that these entities, which accompany either dream visions or waking experiences, are endowed with a degree of independence and autonomy—and, more disturbingly perhaps, a degree of consciousness which appears to be in advance of our own. This is where it becomes difficult to differentiate between projection and independent 'realities', for these may be *impressions* rather than realities as such. Or impressions of a reality beyond what we ordinarily know. Furthermore, these very super-conscious abilities that the UFO entities exhibit may be precisely those same abilities which are presently dormant—untapped—in the human psyche.

Of course, there are many presuppositions about how the universe works, and in what dimensions conscious beings can exist. Spiritualism, of course, posits the notion of alternate dimensions and realms in which independent, conscious entities exist. This is present in the notion of an afterlife; another world or space in which consciousness voyages after the death of the physical body. Certainly, it becomes clear in UFO literature that these denizens occupy an in-between state; rather, they are like Blavatsky's noumenon *becoming* phenomenon. Whatever they are, they clearly can switch between physical and dream realities at will; and, to confound things further, they obfuscate themselves from everyday believability by leaving behind a trail of absurdity and illogic, thus deliberately subverting what we know as a consensus—or categorical—reality.

In this sense, enantiodromia is one of the typical methods of the trickster in folklore. It is the sheer mercurialness of the phenomenon which demands a psychological, as well as phenomenological, approach to unveil both its methods (of unveiling itself) and its meaning and purpose (the reason for its unveiling). We shall return to the concept of enantiodromia. But first, we must clearly understand how Jung's notion of active imagination ties in with Wilson's emphasis on the importance of intentionality.

Metaphors and Meta-Logic

The UFO phenomena—like a Zen kōan or an esoteric secret— may yield to our comprehension but remain fundamentally inexpressible. There is a sense that, to communicate certain meanings, one must turn to symbol and to theatrics, even to dream logic and altered states of consciousness. This is fundamentally the reason why all the fields correspond or cross-fertilise each other; each remains at the periphery of our comprehension and expression. Indeed, there is a sense of an *implicit truth* that lies beyond the veil of what is apparent. Revelations which often accompany the UFO, the kōan and the esoteric insight are often grasped on the threshold of *both* our rational mind and imaginative faculties; it is, therefore, at man's most integrated in which his higher faculties can grasp extraordinary—or super- natural—logic. This is what Wilson meant by achieving a 'bird's- eye view'.

In a previous essay, I wrote: 'Esotericism or the "occult" can perhaps be summarised by this notion of transmuting the conceptually obscured, or hidden nature of reality, into everyday perception. And to do this, of course, is to increase the relationality of consciousness' (Stanley; 2017: 111). This 'step- over' from the super-conscious mind of greater meanings into our conscious understanding *is* the evolution of consciousness. When it happens there is a sense of new relationships between things that previously seemed infinitely and inexplicably separated. Enantiodromia—when things become their opposite—as seen from a 'bird's-eye view' would be perceived for what it is: the 'return of the repressed'; for something *within* consciousness is not being addressed *because* it is neither sensed nor perceived by the lower levels of consciousness. Again, Wilson's statement that 'if the flame of consciousness is low, a symbol has no power to evoke reality' becomes a key to our understanding this concept

(1980: 112).

The UFO—existing in the difficult in-between hinterlands of respectability and reason—appears to be such a symbol itself. Says Jacques Vallée, '[if] you strive to convey a truth that lies beyond the semantic level made possible by your audience's language, you must construct apparent contradictions in terms of ordinary meaning' (2014: 27). Indeed, if the UFO is a symbol that *intends*—assuming it has its own *raison d'être*—to bypass most respectable institutions—and, as Vallée goes on to state, to nevertheless 'implant deep within society far-reaching doubts concerning its basic philosophical tenets'—it must turn itself inside out; that is, by generating its own sense of mystery. Vallée continues, 'it would have to project an image just beyond the belief structure of the target society.' This is what he calls the UFO's 'meta-logic'; precisely the same sort of logic that I have briefly outlined above with Jung's enantiodromia.

Furthermore, there is the metaphorical and analogical nature of the UFO phenomena that appears to generate around it. There is a proliferation of theories, each closely related to the other. Patrick Harpur identifies these as effectively misreading spatial metaphors, in which he goes on to list the analogous connections: 'UFOs come from beyond, inside, outside, next to, above, below, within, etc.' Comparing it to crop circle theory, he extrapolates the analogous connections further: 'extraterrestrial theory: unconscious projection theory :: outer space: inner space :: physical : mental.... extraterrestrial theory: "earth energy" theory :: above: below :: material : immaterial' (2003: 169). One only needs to look at the title of Stan Gooch's excellent book, *Creatures from Inner Space* (1984), for an explicit example of Harpur's observation.

The dramatic and unusual experience of abduction phenomenon as it is reported by many abductees complicates the issue further. As I have mentioned previously, this is one of the subcategories of ufology, and has increasingly dominated the field over sightings of the 'craft' themselves. Indeed, the abduction scenarios often have an intensely dreamlike and apparently non-physical dimension, which further frustrates these spatial and physical-mental juxtapositions. Of course, there is the sense that the UFO and its occupants are interdimensional travellers, utterly at odds with our customs as well as our fundamental experience of time and meaning. Rather like when anthropologists breaching the isolation of ancient tribes, the student—by the very act of integration—affects what it is he wants to observe; rather, it becomes a perceptual as well as cross-cultural mirage of information—in which both sides are quickly confused and misunderstood. To each party the rituals of the other are inevitably misinterpreted—or, indeed, remain altogether incomprehensible. The cultural bridging may take a long time, and even then, the communications may be tenuous and trivial until greater integration is achieved.

EM Forster in his 1924 novel *A Passage to India* depicts a poignant example of this problem when he compares the Englishmen meeting with a group of Hindus, of whom one is requested to sing but, in apparently ignoring the request, continues on with the conversation while intermittently taking sips of tea. As the occasion draws to a close, he suddenly bursts out, 'I may sing now,' and the novel continues:

His thin voice rose, and gave out one sound after another. At times there seemed rhythm, at times there was the illusion of a Western melody. But the ear, baffled repeatedly, soon lost any clue, and wandered in a maze of noises, none harsh or unpleasant, none intelligible. It was the song of an unknown bird. Only the servants understood it... The sounds continued and ceased after a few moments as casually as they had begun—apparently half through a bar, and upon the subdominant.[11]

Of course, this is a basic difference in artistic form, but nevertheless it brings home an important point. Commenting upon this scene the philosopher William Barrett notes that the Westerner may find the 'Oriental music "meaningless"', however, 'the Oriental might very well reply that this is the meaninglessness of nature itself which goes on endlessly without beginning, middle, or end' (1990: 55). Again, the misunderstanding is a philosophical, ontological and even an epistemological one that relates to our understanding of spatial metaphors in regard to time and its processes.

All of this, of course, could be founded upon a series of misconceptions. The phenomenon, baffling as it is—and, as a result, leading us on by analogy to analogy—might yield to our comprehension upon a closer and less severely dualistic framing of our perceptual categories. In fact, upon closer inspection, a sense of an inner-consistency of meaning and purpose seems to underlie much of the phenomenon.

If we accept the idea of a 'deep intentionality' underlying nature, we might say, like Jung, that being born into the physical world is akin to how the unconscious makes itself explicit; that is, being born is nature's unconsciousness (the unmanifest; or potential) becoming explicitly manifest in three-dimensional space—the ordinary world that we find ourselves in, with all its laws and limitations. Jung says that each of us is: '... begotten out of the depths of human nature, or rather out of living Nature herself. It is a personification of vital forces quite outside the limited range of our conscious mind; of ways and possibilities of which our one-sided conscious mind knows nothing; a wholeness which embraces the very depths of Nature.' Jung is here talking about the archetype of the 'child'; however, one could apply this just as well to creativity itself. And, moreover, to those unusual events that frustrate our curiously 'one-sided' consciousness.

Two examples of what Jung called synchronicity will throw light on the problem of understanding these 'meta-logical' events. In each example there is a similar comprehension of information that challenges our notions of time and causality. There is, as it were, an incursion of our fourth-dimensional selves which, born from Nature's unconscious, still exists in this dimension of radically different laws to the physical. We exist in the world most viscerally, but, fundamentally, we are *not of it* entirely.

In *Gifts of Unknown Things* (1976) Lyall Watson relates one of his experiences of travelling through the Amazon, when one of his fellow Brazilian *caboclos* developed an intense toothache. Developing an abscess, the tooth and surrounding gums became inflamed and the man went into a delirious high fever. None of the boat's crew had any access to any antibiotics or painkillers; they simply had to proceed through the Amazon while Watson attempted crude methods such as removing it with a pair of pliers. Giving up, his fellow traveller continued to suffer, when suddenly one of the boatmen suggested they visit a nearby famous healer that lived a few hours further down the river.

The 'great healer' to Watson's astonishment was a 'terrible disappointment', described as a 'small, hungry-looking, middle-aged man with little hair and fewer clothes' sporting only a 'tattered pair of shorts, plastic sandals' and a T-shirt that was once the property of the State Prison of Louisiana (139). Nevertheless, with nothing to lose they presented to the healer the feverish, and no doubt by now delirious, patient. The communication took place in Amazonian-Portuguese and Watson noticed that the emphasis was not on the symptoms, but rather the 'particular circumstances, the exact time and place, they were first noted' (1976: 139). This was a sleight of hand, Watson believed, to reroute the 'blame' on to an external and apparently malevolent entity; a psychological trick, perhaps, to provide some sort of catharsis, or to place the patient into a particular relationship with his suffering.

The procedure began rather bizarrely. In fact, the healer

started to sing to himself, in a native dialect, while he placed his hand into the patient's mouth and began to rummage around, with the occasional grunt, and eventually pulled out the molar with an uncanny ease. The bleeding, as a result, was remarkably slight. And, furthermore, the healer began to sway with his eyes closed, and suddenly, one of the boatmen pointed out that there was a trickle of blood flowing out the corner of the patient's mouth. However, what happened next was far more inexplicable. Suddenly, along the line of trickling blood, emerged a column of black army ants. Watson observed that they were not a frantic, searching set of ants, but a strict regiment following the line of blood and apparently emerging all from the patient's wound. They continued to flow, walking down his body and on to the log on which he was sitting.

Strangely enough, Watson's fellow boatmen began laughing at the spectacle. And yet, 'it was not the nervous laughter of people in fear and discomfort. It was honest loud laughter over something that struck them as very funny' (1976: 141). For, as Watson relates, in the 'local dialect, they use the same word for pain as they do for the army ant. The healer had promised the pain would leave, and so it did *in the form of an elaborate and extraordinary pun*' [my italics] (1976: 141–142).

This second 'synchronicity' is not so dramatic, but what it does have is an analogical quality that frames the above argument well; again, there is a meta-logic about it, and again, the curious sense of humour is present.

Fred Gettings, in *The Secret Lore of the Cat* (1989), describes the curious genesis of his book, which all began with a commission to take photographs of medieval cities in Europe. In doing so, he found himself wandering around the backstreets of Ghent, Belgium. Behind Lange Steenstraat a ginger tom caught his eye—or, more accurately, the ginger tom directed Gettings' attention—by jumping up on to a nearby windowsill. Juxtaposing itself against the lush plant life, red geraniums in terracotta pots;

no doubt an idyllic vision perfect for a photographer. Gettings, grabbing his camera, immediately began to take snapshots of the stylish cat when a young woman appeared in front of his viewfinder, allowing the cat to enter into the house. Noticing that the man outside was interested, she smiled and offered him in for some coffee. It turned out that she was an artist and was, in fact, working on illustrations for a book on cats. This piqued Gettings' interest, who had also written and researched art and art history for many years. Curiously, she suddenly asked whether he had seen the artist Arthur Rackham's depiction of cats. He said he had indeed, and as he did so, she reached over for a book near the windowsill—astonishingly, it was *the* book on Arthur Rackham which he had written over a decade before.

Gettings muses: 'What a magical cat her ginger tom had been to draw me with such cunning into his owner's house. That cat had not really been interested in having his photograph taken —he merely had access to the secret wisdom, and knew that his mistress and I should meet, talk about cats, Rackham and life.' He continues by saying that long after the event he, '... could not get the ginger out of my mind. I knew already that the cat is a magical creature, with an arcane symbolism special to itself, yet I had never before become personally entangled in the feline magic it can weave.' And yet why is the cat so different?—Why, he asked himself, was the cat so important to the Egyptians and witchcraft and so on. Of course, this all led to the writing of *The Secret Lore of the Cat*.

Both of these cases of synchronicity are in keeping with the meta-logic of the UFO experience, although the UFO experience, in comparison with these essentially mild synchronicities, is far more intensive.

The sort of physical punning that takes place in Lyall Watson's account is very interesting, for it presupposes that the healer works simultaneously on many levels—psychological as well as physical. In fact, the two worlds blend together seamlessly.

Firstly there is the ritual or suggestion that one ought to displace the problem by attributing it some 'outside' force, or embodying the issue as the workings of some malignant entity. Secondly, there is the apparent ease of the extraction and curious lack of blood—there is a sense that he can, to some degree, command matter itself. And, thirdly, there is the symbolic bleeding of the ants that related directly to the boatmen's language; that is, the ants are etymologically linked with the word 'pain'. Normally, if this story was told to someone it would appear to be entirely symbolic—and yet, Watson apparently witnessed it first hand. This is typical of the UFO experience; particularly in regards to the bizarre abduction accounts that are often recounted in books like Strieber's *Communion* (1987).

Jung, speaking of the UFO, believes that they are in fact:

> impressive manifestations of totality whose simple, round form portrays the archetype of the self, which as we know from experience plays the chief role in uniting apparently irreconcilable opposites and is therefore best suited to compensate the split-mindedness of the age. (2002: 17)

Interestingly, one could posit two realities that intertwine, and that the reality of the 'symbolic reality' is not entirely separate. Indeed, this explains the synchronicity phenomena as well as the effect of enantiodromia; the one becomes the other—not because they are separated, or indeed polar opposites—but because the dimensions of the other 'half', so to speak, are interlaced with an aspect of experienced reality. The 'totality' of a synchronicity seems to play this out too, for the healer performs a ritual that is both symbolic *and* physical; that is, the synchronicity—such as in Gettings' case—is both a message—an interpreted meaning— and *simultaneously* an unfolding of inexplicably related events. A universe constituted of meaningful connections would, in fact, have this curious quality of interplay between its dimensions.

The synchronicity is a sort of 'weighted meaning' that drops down into reality, and, as it blends with the laws of our ordinary dimension of lived experience, *acts itself out as a series of events.* To use another analogy, it is rather like an ice crystal forms into a network of symmetrical shapes on the window; firstly, it crystallizes, hardens, and then begins to take form from its previous, less tangible form of liquid or gas. In a Platonic sense, it is as the evolutionary philosopher, Henri Bergson, says: 'The possible would have been there from all time, a phantom awaiting its hour; it would therefore have become reality by the addition of something, by some transfusion of blood or life' — or, in this case, manifesting as events latent with metaphor.

Again, Madame Blavatsky in *The Secret Doctrine* makes a similar point: 'Neither the form of man, nor that of any animal, plant or stone, has ever been "created", and it is only on this plane of ours that it commenced "becoming", that is to say, objectivizing into its present materiality, or expanding *from within outwards*, from the most sublimated and supersensuous essence into its grossest appearance.' This appearance, of course, is the phenomenal world of the senses. Synchronicities, too, seem to expand from *within outwards*, becoming both an event and simultaneously an inner-sense of meanings lying *outside of time.*

Gettings' case is more explicit and simple; the cat simply leads him to a fortuitous meeting that resulted in a creative as well as intellectual endeavour. Whether or not this was the cat's intention is beside the point — although one could suppose that the cat, like Watson's ants, could be guided by some deeper current of meaning than we yet understand. A synchronicity, if it involves an object, or a unique arrangement of events etc., presupposes that meaning can somehow organise apparently chaotic matter into aggregation of interconnected, meaningful 'events'. Indeed, they may remind us that each moment is pregnant with blossoming potential, and, when we feel sufficiently relaxed or acutely perceptive, we can perceive this apparent miraculous nature of the present moment. Now, did the cat know what it was doing? Probably not. But as it is perhaps more deprived of free will than man, it can in some sense be a part of the background of an 'intentionality principle'. To speculate further, one could say that Gettings' 'transcendental ego' telepathically utilised the cat to set up a series of complex interactions!

Nevertheless, the cat for Gettings' became a living symbol—and not only for himself, as he found out, but that it had always been interpreted as a symbol of unseen forces throughout time. In fact, he includes in his book an image of a cat adorned with the Egyptian symbol of the Udjat (the eye of Horus), otherwise known as The Gayer-Anderson Cat now found in the British Museum. He goes on to ask the question, 'Are occultists wrong in claiming that this Udjat is the symbol of the so-called "third eye", that organ of higher vision which is as yet undeveloped in ordinary men?' Furthermore, he presents a brief history of this eye: 'Horus was the king-god whose eyes were associated with luminaries—his right eye with the Sun, his left eye with the Moon', and similarly that the 'left' and 'right' motifs were symbolised in two lions which 'posted on the couchant on either side of the large solar symbol of Horus, the sun-god' representing, respectively, the past (left) and the future (right)—and, more significantly for this essay, *a point which lies outside of time* (1989: 27).

Of course, there is an immense amount of analogous thinking required to see these events in such a deeply meaningful way. And if, indeed, either of these synchronistic events truly happened as reported, we can see why they would affect the witnesses so deeply. Indeed, it took Lyall Watson years to openly admit his experience with the Amazonian healer. And Fred Gettings devoted an entire book in an attempt to unravel the mystery of the cat as a mythological as well as an esoteric symbol.

Implicit in Gettings' conclusions is the interesting awareness of the hemispheric functioning of the brain. Turning to Egyptian symbolism Gettings is able to navigate himself into a new way of seeing; the cat is just one of many metaphors that remind us of these significant perceptual differences. Time, of course, has a primary role to play in synchronicities, for the event takes place in an unusual contradiction of meaning influencing time and space; the event is so significant due to its apparent transcendence of time. In each instance a deeply meaningful synchronicity happens such that there is a sense that time and space are not what they appear to be; in fact, we suspect that reality as we experience it works on a whole new set of principles previously overlooked. Again, this has much in common with the UFO experience. It seems to work on the same principle: that of a reminder; or as a phenomenon deliberately 'churning' up our preconceptions of time and space, rather like a plough heaving up the soil for the season's new growths to flourish.

Now, regards time and space the two hemispheres of the brain function differently. Each has its unique processing mechanism when it comes to meaning, interpretation of sequence, and each even has a predisposition to either order or chaos: analytical logic or 'lateral' thinking. In fact, speaking generally the left hemisphere has a preference for orderliness, routine and predictability, whereas the right is quite at home in the fuzzy world of analogy and metaphor, timelessness and unusual juxtapositions. In other words, the synchronicity and the UFO, *as an experience*, would be accommodated by the right brain and rejected, perhaps, by the left brain. Jordan Peterson in his recent Bible series lectures even went so far as to suggest that the brain, roughly divided, can be mapped on to dualistic dynamics such as order and chaos, light and dark etc.[12] This can best be symbolised by the Yin and Yang symbol, in which a small section of each is situated at the heart of the other. That is, as both have strictly delineated frontiers, there is nevertheless an aspect—or an essence—present in each respective territory.

Fundamentally it is a dynamic, with its two oppositions forming a creative cooperation rather than mutual destruction.

In essence the interplay between two hemispheres—or two 'essences' as found in Jung's concept of enantiodromia— becomes a type of switching between opposites, or, in which something becomes inside out or upside down; our perceptions flip over and suddenly another aspect, which we had overlooked before, seems palpably self-evident. This is what I meant when I said that *the central dictum of esoteric philosophy is to transmute the conceptually obscured into a conscious sense of deeper meanings.* The incursion of unusual and anomalous events is precisely the challenge to at least one of our perceptual mechanisms, and the only way in which to unravel its logic—the logic of a synchronicity or a mystical revelation—is to balance the two hemispheric processes of the brain; to recalibrate what Kant's categories obscure, that is, *the noumenal is only unknowable to one half of our perceptual systems.*

In fact, each hemisphere has difficulty knowing great swathes of the other's capacities and capabilities—each half is in a sense alienated from the other. What are for one side phenomena remains inaccessible—noumenon—to the other; so, to transcend this self-limiting boundary dispute, they must work in a harmonic and dynamic tandem. And if they did, synchronicities would become commonplace. Our existence would become populated by the esoteric concept of 'the language of the birds', a language that allows direct communication and understanding of the deeper dimensions of reality—a reality usually occulted from our normal perceptual systems.

Now, back in 2009, when I asked Colin Wilson what he'd recommend to someone who is an incorrigible pessimist like Louis-Ferdinand Céline, his answer was somewhat uncharacteristic. Usually sceptical about drugs (read the appendix to *Beyond the Outsider*, for example), Wilson nevertheless relayed an insight he obtained from RH Ward, who wrote the 1957 book,

A Drug-Taker's Notes. Of course someone like Céline would be completely sealed off to meaning, for he had made it a habit to discredit everything as ultimately meaningless, and viewed the world cynically. To regain this sort of 'meaning perception' would have been very difficult for Céline, and Wilson's answer was to suggest some sort of experience that would change his mind. Wilson quotes at length RH Ward in *The Occult* (1971):

Last night as I was walking home from the station I had one of those strange experiences of 'rising up within oneself', of 'coming inwardly alive' ... A minute or so after I had left the station, I was attacked... by indigestion... I thought to myself, though I suppose not in so many words, 'I could separate myself from this pain; it belongs only to my body and is real only to the physical not-self. There is no need for the self to feel it.' Even as I thought this the pain disappeared; that is, it was in some way left behind because I, or the self, had gone somewhere where it was not; and the sensation of 'rising up within' began...

First there is the indescribable sensation in the spine, as of *something mounting up*, a sensation which is partly pleasure and partly awe, a physical sensation and yet one which, if it makes sense to say so, is beginning to be not physical. This was accompanied by an extraordinary feeling of *bodily lightness*, of well-being and effortlessness, as if one's limbs had no weight and one's flesh had been suddenly transmuted into some rarer substance. But it was also, somehow, a feeling of living more in the upper part of one's body than the lower, a certain peculiar awareness of one's head as... the most important and intelligent of one's members. There was also a realization that one's facial expression was changing; the eyes were wider open than usual; the lips were involuntarily smiling. Everything was becoming 'more', everything was *going up on to another level...*

I found that I could think in a new way. Or rather, it would be more accurate to say that I could think-and-feel in a new way, for it was hard to distinguish between thought and feeling… *This was like becoming possessed of a new faculty.* (Quoted in Wilson; 1988: 736–737.)

Everything 'becoming more' is also what Wilson called 'relationality' or 'Faculty X'; that ability to connect meanings until an almost overwhelming sense of infinite meaningfulness rekindles and vivifies our perceptual—and intentional—fires. *In this state each meaning, symbol and metaphor become intrinsically evolutionary.* When the 'flame of consciousness is low, a symbol has no power to evoke reality, and intellect is helpless.' A feeling of the relationality—as opposed to a feeling of the unrelated and diffuse world of a pessimist, or someone who is tired—is precisely the opposite; instead, for them, reality is grasped by an active intentionality, yielding further to a fuller and richer comprehension, or, as Alfred North Whitehead called it, *prehension* (the ability to grasp meaning). Suddenly, says Wilson of Faculty X, one would become intensely aware of 'other times and other places'. Indeed, this is what RH Ward also calls the sensation of 'becoming possessed of a new faculty'.

This faculty enables a new cosmological vision of our role in space and time, and moreover enables a direct perception of the underlying meanings inherent in the evolutionary process. For example, in his book *The Paranormal*, Stan Gooch paints a picture of a living cosmos in which '"spirit" takes a huge step forward' by cloaking itself in the material world, for now it can 'operate at an infinitely more meaningful level. It is now in a position (as ever, from outside "space") to upgrade its broadcast transmissions—the transmission of itself into "space". Far more complex and more purposeful messages now become possible' (1978: 297). Phenomena such as UFOs and synchronicity, it could be argued, are this meaningful level of spirit partaking in the phenomenal world, upgrading, to use Gooch's terms, the 'broadcast transmissions' by expanding the witness' understanding of the universal laws in which he lives. Gooch argues that these evolutionary faculties—RH Ward's vision, Faculty X and others—are *preformed* or latent potentialities for the evolution of man's consciousness. And what is so curious is that these very 'magical' faculties seem to exist in the transcendental ego, that super-conscious element in our psyche which appears to hold the key to our conscious evolution. Indeed, this is what Wilson meant when he said that the 'first man to learn the secret of the control of consciousness will be the first true man, wholly in possession of the new dimension of freedom' (1972: 150). Not only that, he will become the superman; man *in his entire potential*.

But the question remains: what leads us onwards and upwards? Goethe says it's the 'eternal feminine'; for Wilson and Husserl it is the transcendental ego; for Madame Blavatsky it is the interplay between noumena and phenomena; and in Watson's *Miracle Visitors* it is the 'inaccessibilities' that tease out our greatest mental leaps. In a sense they're all aspects of each other, bleeding over seamlessly into one another's territory; eternally presenting a sort of meta-logical game that challenges our presumptions every time we become too complacent. Arthur M. Young captured this nature of the universal game in the title of his 1976 book, *The Reflexive Universe*. Similarly to Watson and Vallée he presents a theory of a 'metalanguage', which has been described elsewhere as a requirement: '... for any evolving system, a pattern that can help to illuminate man's destiny in the universe and instruct the process of individual and social transformation. In deciphering the universal kōan of process... [representing] the beginnings of a metalanguage for the higher-order paradigm shift that is so urgently required at this stage of human evolution.'

This sort of odd logic that we have explored is at the heart of esotericism and the occult—with such logic present in synchronicities described above. I've here chosen to refer to these experiences as exercises in providing mankind with a series of *evolutionary metaphors*.

Evolutionary Metaphors

Evolutionary metaphors—along with esoteric 'correspondences' and the logic of much anomalous phenomenon—baffle ordinary causal logic precisely by transcending its limits and by *inferring beyond itself*. Essentially they are symbols of a reality yet to *become*. Indeed, to understand the evolutionary metaphor's ambiguous nature we must develop imaginative as well as supra-logical faculties which can process this level of reality from which these metaphors emerge, and in doing so, it would be immediately grasped that they can become more than mere symbols *but actualities*. In this sense one realises that the meaning for something *becoming* must first reside as an *implicit possibility*— and only upon its explication does it become manifestly real. One might think of this process in terms of the Big Bang, for indeed, the whole universe was implicitly possible within the first billionths of a second. Although, as we shall see, time itself provides another level of complexity regarding the emergence of what was previously implicit.

We are, quite literally, within two minds regarding our cosmological picture. For it is in these elevated states of mind, as in moments of Faculty X, and other forms of 'relational consciousness', that we are capable of grappling with these 'higher order' incursions into our lives. Furthermore, this directly relates to our perception of meaning in our everyday lives, for we remain, to an extent, limited within the lower rungs of the hierarchical structure of consciousness. And at the lower levels, of course, meaning itself becomes more diffuse, less relational and resultantly two-dimensional and relative—that is, without any qualitatively 'higher' or 'lower' aspect.

These various levels of consciousness, which Wilson called the 'ladder of selves', enable us to see a direct correlation between the diffuse and 'meaningless' states of consciousness in contrast to the integrated sense of related meanings. Indeed, with each ascent of the 'ladder', a degree of integration occurs in the psyche which enables a comprehension of the interrelated nature of reality, and, therefore, the underlying sense of purpose and meaning of existence. Understanding this, of course, provides an essential reason for increasing our consciousness, for it enables us to see lower states as more disconnected from the truth than the higher states and, furthermore, that the intentional nature of consciousness in itself implies to what degree objective meaning is *grasped and integrated.*

Fundamentally it is this recognition that consciousness is, in relation to meaning, *active* rather than passive, which in itself opens up an interesting approach to the anomalous. The evolutionary metaphor, in this sense, guides consciousness towards an increasing development of its higher faculties, goading the mind up the 'ladder of selves' towards a more inclusive sense of reality. Mysteries, after all, are simply those realities we have not yet understood, and with each increase of our knowledge, mysteries become less mysterious, but not necessarily any less marvellous.

A certain invigoration and mental healthiness comes with the recognition of large-scale meanings, for example, in a religious vision of a divinely purposeful life. Again this directly relates to Wilson's idea of the 'bird's-eye view' as opposed to the close-up, and diminished 'worm's-eye view'. Furthermore, one *infers*, by its very premises, that there is something beyond ordinary everyday existence; in other words, the metaphor refers to something beyond itself. A metaphor, of course, can either be a symbol or merely a figure of speech, even a comparison or, in its more complex form, a poem or mimesis. Nevertheless, a metaphor can sometimes clarify something that is expressed too explicitly — and metaphor in fact 'embodies' the issue by example, likeness or correspondence, even providing an empathic bridge.

If we take metaphor as a form of imitation, or indeed, a

mimesis of one level of reality in symbolic form—inferring as it does something outside of itself, yet nevertheless relating to a reality as such—we may begin to see it as a form of what Iain McGilchrist calls an *'imaginative inhabiting of the other'*, which, he argues, is 'always different because of its intersubjective betweenness.' These 'empathic bridges' are drawn across by 'intention, aspiration, attraction and empathy, drawing heavily on the right hemisphere [of the brain], whereas copying is the following of disembodied procedures and algorithms, and is left-hemisphere based' (2009: 249). By contrast, of course, the left hemisphere merely copies, and the right, being more theatrical and symbolical, prefers the evolutionary metaphor which unifies the thing it is mimicking within a symbolic reality which incorporates more levels of relational meaning than a literal-minded representation. McGilchrist argues that the survival values of this sort of thinking are immense, for they would encourage social cohesion and increase the transfer of symbolic—therefore embodied—information between individuals. In fact, the symbol or metaphor is more universal than explicit, analytical language, for this is in fact a much later development both historically and, importantly, biologically.

A 'magical' consciousness is not necessarily at odds with reality; in fact, due to its gestalt-like nature, it can absorb far more information than a careful, analytical approach. For example, Bronislaw Malinowski's 1914 research into the Trobriand Islanders highlighted the fact that ritual, although being rather 'irrational' from a Westerner's point of view, nevertheless proved the South Sea fishermen seemed to flourish due to a general sense of *control*, even if, fundamentally, this control was an 'illusory' ritual from the point of view of science. Embedded in the ritual was an accurate understanding of reality, and therefore the ritual provided the necessary symbol for the transmission of the fruitful and constructive activity. Howard Bloom in *The Lucifer Principle* (1998) concludes that '[this] belief in magic is one clue to our need for memes. Religious and scientific schemes—clusters of guesswork that sometimes seem like a madman's dreams—offer the feeling of control, an indispensable fuel for the physiological powerhouses of life' (114).

To switch to more recent times, it is curious to note that during these times of upheaval and unrest, memes, defined as 'virally-transmitted cultural symbol or social idea', and now a (sometimes) amusing Internet phenomenon, should spread both to entertain, but also, to provide a semblance of symbolic understanding—or control—by condensing information into a compacted and easily digestible 'punch line'. If something irritates or baffles someone, there is usually a corresponding meme which aims to represent the illogicality of a political, personal, or social phenomenon. Rather like the Trobriand Islanders, there is a sense that the 'meme' in the chaotic environment of the Internet is becoming a means to navigate the unpredictable world of information. In a strange sort of way the Internet—a now extremely rich bed of information—generates a type of mythological consciousness, although this is in its earliest and crudest stages.

With the advent of the Internet, with its visual and information-rich as well interactive nature, we have once again stepped back into an unusual situation in which the 'metaphorical' consciousness may once again thrive. That is, now our culture has become complex in terms of its sheer speed of information transfer, we are reconfiguring the way we attend to the world and our psyche. Borders, in a sense, have been crossed, and distance itself is reduced; communication and cultural ideas can leap bounds, and instantly spread throughout the world in a matter of hours, even minutes. This is reflected in news reportage and so on, and even with freak events which are circulated at the speed of light through optic cable.

In this new climate of what the late sociologist Zygmunt Bauman called 'liquid modernity' bonds are tied evermore delicately, allowing for an immediate, on-call flexibility to accommodate the ever-shifting sands of an information-saturated culture.

In recent times we have had to reconfigure our cultural thermostat, integrating new and evermore flexible and experimental techniques to somehow 'embed' the information into a context that can provide a discernible and meaningful shape to our world. The symbol, the imagistic condensation into a meme, has become a sort of recombinational 'search mechanism' for meaning. Of course, such a cultural environment sets itself up rather well for the reintroduction of a form of magical consciousness, in which images and memes can be used to navigate and control a chaotic environment. Indeed, the language which we use is increasingly orientated towards information, relativism and therefore provides a backdrop in which, once again, the symbol or intent can cross over between language—words—and the image. Nevertheless, it is still too early to fully embrace all of the potential evolutionary implications of a culture so saturated with information fed through a form of media which incorporates all previous mediums.

As a result of this new world of information, the emergence of chaos magic, as I mentioned briefly in the first chapter, takes its stake in the new 'magical consciousness', taking advantage as it does of the postmodern juxtaposition of unusual and experimental points-of-view and harnessing the symbol as a means of codifying magical intent—their will to power over a world composed of information.

Now, what we might be seeing in the modern world is the re-emergence of a type of magical thinking that had previously gone underground, so to speak, or had remained dormant in the unconscious regions of our collective psyche. And yet, evolutionary metaphors such as the UFO, synchronicities and flashes of revelatory consciousness seem further away than ever. The cultural zeitgeist tends to diminish the metaphysical—and therefore metaphorical—impulses that constitute the balance and integration of a healthy and dynamical mind. As our culture is becoming increasingly politicized, it, as a result, tends towards a subjugation of the individual, replacing a type of group-think that can easily result out of an intensely socially-networked world. Inner revolutions seem rarer than outer, political ones. The self, as a result, becomes increasingly low-resolution, reduced to a sort of caricature or a simplistic image-based vignette composed of shallow surfaces. This, of course, has increased our left hemisphere's predilection to what McGilchrist describes as the 'following of disembodied procedures and algorithms.'[13]

In terms of the UFO phenomenon, Jung pronounced that its message, at least in dream symbolism, is intended so that *everybody* should be aware of their existence by appearing in the sky, but, crucially, they *'bid each of us remember his own soul and his own wholeness, because this is the answer the West should give to the danger of mass-mindedness'* [my italics] (2002: 81). Curiously, and significantly, the UFO for Jung reminds us of our individuality, and for many people who witness the phenomena, one can certainly say that it is a disturbing and unique experience as is evident in many of the witness accounts. Although there are cases in which there is an instilled ecological consciousness, and a sense of planetary responsibility, there is also the element of individual psychic and psychological development brought about by the experience itself.

Here we may turn to the philosophy as outlined in Wilson's Outsider Cycle, for again it leads us back to the problem he addresses in the first book of the series, *The Outsider*. The individual, stricken by an existential vision, who nevertheless consciously or unconsciously strives towards a form of psychological integration. Wilson's outsider, of course, is in revolt against mass-mindedness, and instead requires for himself an independent and unique vision of something objective — in other words, something that resides outside of the limits of reductionism and the confining, ultimately pessimistic boundaries of postmodern culture. However, as Lachman emphasises, the outsider's 'problems are not his alone; they involve all of civilization.' He continues: 'Western civilization [has] reached a dead end... and it could only move on if the Outsiders, the men and women of vision and purpose, overcame their uncertainty, *ceased to be Outsiders*, and imposed their values on the world around them' (2016: 66–67).

At this point we might ask ourselves, 'What values should the Outsider impose?' and for this, we might consider the abductees or UFO witnesses, who, with their normal preconceptions about existence and its possibilities challenged—or even explicitly modified directly by the experience itself—naturally pose a new vision in which time, space and the meaning constituted out of these constants may be turned on its head. Now, whether one *becomes* an Outsider, in Wilson's meaning of the word, by undergoing these experiences is difficult to argue, for many considerations of the cases individually would have to be examined in tandem to the Outsider Cycle.

Wilson's Outsiders, of course, essentially recognised in themselves greater forces than mere personality, and that they were in a sense channels for an archetypal and fundamentally impersonal life force. And if like Stan Gooch we take the UFO, science fiction and the field of the paranormal as a vast arrangement of preformed evolutionary potentialities, as it were, we can begin to see each glimpse into these alternative realities as vision into evolutionary multiplicities, its implicit 'realities' yet to become, and furthermore, into its underlying vitality.

In many of the Outsiders as well as the abductees, there is a vision of a new modality of being that infers meaning that is fundamentally practical and personal, and, once actualised *in the individual*, becomes applicable to society-at-large. In recognising the essentially creative nature of the experience, whether in the visions of the Outsider or in the traumatic yet simultaneously revelatory quality in the works of Whitley Strieber, we may perceive the outline of a new way of understanding of time in order to reorientate our relationship to *meaning*. Again, here one is reminded of Wilson's Faculty X, for Strieber came to realise that we need to 'unlearn the assumption that the future is in front of us, the present is where we are, and the past is behind us.' Strieber continues:

> That is a false view of time. The visitors offer a much better idea of time. They say the future is to the right, and it's like water. The present is here and now, and it's like a compressor. And the past is like ice. The water has now been turned into ice because the present has decided the shape the water will take, the shape the past will take. And this leaves room for entry into many different possible futures. We can change that water into any number of different shapes simply by the way we address it... What we have to learn to do—and this is as much an inner movement as an artefact of some potential technology—is to learn to move out of the time stream so that we can examine it more carefully and come to understand its real meaning.[14]

Implicit in this realisation of the reality of 'other times and places' man can act in a far more constructive way, and see himself as fundamentally important in the actualisation of realities in the stream of time. Again, the evolutionary metaphor is what the Kabbalists call *tikkun*, a repairing symbol that bridges the visible world with the invisible, and vice versa. Emphasising the nature of time along the same lines of Strieber, Lachman describes this process in *Caretakers*:

> When we 'complete' the world, when we 'represent' the 'unrepresented', when we infuse dead matter with meaning, *when we fill the empty forms of reality with the living force of the imagination*, we are moving against the tide that is carrying

the fallen, physical world into nothingness. (2013: 221)
Ultimately, the later view is *entropic*: it tends towards decay
and disorder. Whereas the former, 'infusing dead matter
with meaning', is *negentropic*: tending towards order and
meaningfulness. Here Lachman emphasises the 'filling up' of the
material universe with implicit meanings which work against
entropy and time's one-directional arrow.

Now there are two poignant symbols of both our
understanding of a cosmos—a whole unified meaning—and
a chaos, or that which results out of imbalance, allowing in
destructive and destabilizing qualities. Jung's discovery of the
mandala in effect symbolises man's inner-cosmos, his psyche,
into the artistic creation of a whole with a centre—a centre
which symbolises man's point of individuation. The mandala
is an artistic image, usually colourful and which is orientated
around a central point, usually pulling inwards, as it were, all
of the outside images; it is an attempt to spontaneously express
the unconscious and conscious forces into a representative
image of one's inner-being. Usually, but not necessarily always
symmetrical, it emphasises the psychic working of an individual,
and particularly lays emphasis on integration of the Self. This
is significantly in contrast to the chaos magic symbol, which is
orientated *outwards* towards a magic form assertion (below):

Referred to as post-modern magic, or indeed 'pop magic', it is
symbolised almost entirely by *externalized* influences, with little

emphasis on interiority. As a modern phenomenon, on the fringes, it nevertheless represents a current of occult thinking in modern times. One commentator, the comic book artist Grant Morrison, mentions briefly the notion of a 'hyper sigil', a symbolic image which represents for the magician some will of which he wants to exert on to the world around him. The 'hyper sigil' is a larger version of an ordinary 'sigil', and for Morrison, 'incorporates elements such as characterization, drama and plot. The hyper sigil is a sigil extended through the fourth dimension.'[15] In other words, it is a dramatic cultural shift willed and enacted—or represented—through a cultural medium such as art, music or, in this case, Morrison's imaginative comic books.

This type of experimental cultural manipulation is due to the fact that, as Peter Carroll says, 'for the first time in history we live in a world where a substantial fraction of humanity has freedom of belief, and hardly knows what to do with it', and this means that postmodernist, post-monotheist 'culture has yet to formally explicate its ideal spirituality' (2008: 55). This is where chaos magick steps in. Further on in *The Apophenion* he discusses a type of neo-pantheism which attempts to provide both an animistic and meaningful interaction with the environment. Uniquely, he places emphasis on the practicality of 'magical thinking', disposing it if it fails to work, and integrating it into its system of practices if it fails. Underlying his thesis, there appears to be no overarching metaphysic, or, in a sense, an evolutionary purpose— it is simply an experimental framework towards the rebuilding of a magical, metaphorical and analogical—even imaginal— worldview. He continues, '… if a superstition gives good results it gets reused, and coincidence rarely gets dismissed as mere coincidence… So if a synchronicity appears spontaneously we should consider interpreting it as an affirmation of deep intent, or a warning from the subconscious' (2008: 60). And, as we have seen in the idea of 'deep intentionality', here Carroll acknowledges a similar 'metaphysic' in the sense of what he calls 'deep intent' — this, essentially, is the closest chaos magic gets to an overall evolutionary 'metaphysic'. In essence, Peter Carroll's 'chaos magic paradigm' has its roots in phenomenology, for it incorporates direct experience based on its effectiveness and an active and creative relationship with reality.

Although there is a psychological dimension to chaos magic, what it is lacking is a vision of integration, of an emphasis on inner development. For example, when it posits the value of analogical thinking, it also understates the dangers of being misled. Ritual magicians warned precisely against these and projected — like Lyall Watson's Amazonian healer — the psychological dangers into disembodied entities or ritual and symbolic situations. What this did was to contextualize the issue into something *concrete*; that is, they were explicitly reminding themselves that it had to be dealt with practically and *as if* it were an objective reality. This emphasis on objective consciousness — by stepping back from oneself — enabled the individual to discipline his own mind by refusing to be 'taken in' by a distorting web of entanglements produced by negative emotions — produced either in the individual or a collective malaise present in the ritual atmosphere, or even culture, at large.

However, the philosophical and existential insights of chaos magic cannot be underestimated. Indeed, its relativisms — as can be seen in the idea of neo-pantheism — may seem to undermine any particular philosophical or religious foundation, instead celebrating ambiguity and the 'meaning perception's' ability to make models, new juxtapositions and heady brews of associative thinking. Nevertheless, there is also the element of Alfred North Whitehead's statement that: 'Speculative philosophy... is the endeavour to frame a coherent, logical, necessary system of general ideas in terms of which every element of our experience can be interpreted.' Certainly, Whitehead's definition of experience expands over a wide range of states:

Nothing can be omitted, experience drunk and experience sober, experience sleeping and experience waking, experience drowsy and experience wide-awake, experience self-conscious and experience self-forgetful, experience intellectual and experience physical, experience religious and experience sceptical, experience anxious and experience care-free, experience anticipatory and experience retrospective, experience happy and experience grieving, experience dominated by emotion and experience under self-restraint, experience in the light and experience in the dark, experience normal and experience abnormal.[16]

It is from this gestalt of experience that one can begin to make a new model of the cosmos that man finds himself an important part. It provides a working hypothesis in which one can act out freedom; it provides, as it were, a fundamental set of axioms from which to actively participate in a reality that tends towards greater complexification and, finally, actualisations of the realities implicit in that complexity. Prototypal models—if they are successful of course—go on to become commonplace tools, whether they are cars, light bulbs, helicopters etc. Again, this was the central insight that drove Arthur M. Young to write about cosmology after he invented the helicopter, for he knew, practically and philosophically, that cosmological models are important for the development of novel ideas and, furthermore, life-enhancing psychological changes. He also intuitively realised that *consciousness itself* is a fundamental part of the cosmos we inhabit, for each evolutionary leap in consciousness is proportional to increased freedom. Young perceived the universe as the declension of light—with its boundless freedom from time and space—into matter, and then, at 'the turn' (or 'shock', as Gurdjieff would have called it), an increasing complexity of organisms—from mineral to man—until man's higher destiny is reflected back at him in the cosmos itself. This is referred to in the ancient hermetic dictum: As above, so below.

It is now worth turning once again to the evolutionary metaphor along with the UFO and its associated phenomena. We will return to the discussion of chaos magic in this new context.

In his book *Passport to the Cosmos* (1999) the psychologist and parapsychologist, John E. Mack, describes the effects of the abduction phenomenon as an 'intrusion into our reality from other realms' that aid and contribute to 'the gradual... spiritual rebirth taking place in Western culture.' Mack continues:

Each of the principal elements of the phenomenon—the traumatic intrusions; the reality-shattering encounters; the energetic intensity; the apocalyptic ecological confrontations; the reconnection with Source; and the forging of new relationships across a dimensional divide—contributes to the *daishigyo*, the great ego death, that is marking the end of the materialist... paradigm that has lost its compatibility with life in the world as we know it. (1999: 299)

In Mack's terms, the UFO experience provides a transformational paradigm in which an individual is rather forcibly reminded of their existential position in a cosmological context. Of course, this is in its broadest possible interpretation. Merely as a phenomenological event—perceived *as if it were real*—it is presented in science-fiction terms, that is, providing a framework in which to examine mankind's purpose and, moreover, the responsibility of the individual in relation to the universe in which he lives. *The experience is always future orientated in the extreme.* Again, like Whitehead's brand of existentialism, one may include the UFO as a symbol for the expansion of understanding ourselves. This, of course, is the sort of thing Jung understood to a great extent, being one of the most formidable intellects to apply himself to the phenomenon.

Whether we accept the UFO as an evolutionary metaphor

or not, it can at least be incorporated and integrated more efficiently if it is treated as such. The phenomenon's demand of multifaceted interpretations offers us the equivalent of a puzzle, an imaginative game, in which one can perceive new patterns, and radically stretch our intellectual, theoretical and imaginative capabilities. Even after a life of directly experiencing and writing about the UFO and abduction phenomenon, Whitley Strieber concludes his lifetime of experience suggests that we are much more than 'sparks in flesh doomed to die with the inevitable implosion of the body' and that, indeed, 'we have hardly even begun to touch on the complexity and enormity of what it is to be human' (2016: 336). He argues that the whole experience energizes a question—that *raison d'être* behind the evolutionary metaphor—which, he argues, is 'our most valuable asset and our best hope' (2016: 336). There is a suggestion in Strieber's response to the 'power of the question', in which mystery in itself ensures the health of a species, for it encourages a growth towards a further understanding of itself and the cosmos.

Now, there is the post-modernism of chaos magic and the relativistic—or endlessly relativising—nature that underlies much of modern culture. The esoteric, of course, is also a part of this culture, but found on the fringes—or, as is sometimes the case, subtly embedded in popular culture such as comic books, films and so on. Its presence is notable in some way, either consciously or unconsciously. Again, chaos magic posits itself as a 'new paradigm' in which to update magic for the 21st century; or, at least, as a psychological tool that incorporates belief in paranormal abilities, inter-dimensional entities or extrasensory powers. Generally speaking, it does not entertain a radical metaphysics that is entirely departed from materialism; its substrate, interestingly, is still basically materialistic in the sense that it relativises Gods, demons, succubae etc. For many chaos magicians these are merely 'animated' psychological projections,

garbed in symbols and dramas that make them appear as real—
or, for practical and ritual purposes, *quasi-independent interactive psychological realities.*

Chaos magic, it could be argued, is a result of the chaos of a world with all its symbols uprooted; drifting and displaced; divorced from a *central* meaning of deeper purpose. To contrast this with Wilson's description of the outsider presents an unusual insight into the modern civilized psyche and the plight of an essentially religious individual.

He is the creative individual whose instinct is to bring order out of chaos, to question the foundations of society... But since the Outsider's impulse is fundamentally religious—the desire to be more 'serious' than other people is the essence of religion—he tends to be less of a misfit in ages of faith than in ages of materialism and skepticism. (1979: 265)

Further on in *Mysteries*, Wilson goes on to discuss UFOs, in which he makes the interesting comment: 'Our minds are essentially provincial when, ideally, they ought to be cosmopolitan. We are not merely earth-bound; we have our heads buried in the earth.' Wilson proceeds to cite Vallée's belief that the 'UFO phenomenon... [is] forcing us to look up, to get used to the idea that we are citizens of the universe, not just of this earth' (1979: 563). This, of course, is the basic religious impulse that plagues the outsider; he feels that ordinary existence is too provincial—that rut of materialism and scepticism—and that this desire for 'seriousness' is essentially a requirement for a larger context which assents man's position as significant—and, moreover, requires of us our active participation in a vast evolutionary project.

Again, Peter J. Carroll in *The Octavo* (2011) recognises that our civilization has reached a degree of immense complexity, some of which he describes as an 'interdependent system of

Integrated Information' created from fossil fuels and other materials. This, he argues, has come to the point where it has run into a diminishing of its returns. However, mirroring this, he recognises that the individual too works on similar 'inputs'. 'We must look for new horizons and boundaries to change our energy/information input. We can use the input to increase our Integrated Information either in quantity or quality, or we can just squander it away on entropy' (2011: 135–136). The outsider's yearning for 'seriousness' is the yearning, essentially, for qualitative meaning and purpose that merits and benefits from — while complementing and elevating — the material manifold of existence. This, essentially, is what Lachman meant when he said the outsider is demanded to impose his values upon the world, for if he declines to do this the values of negentropy and chaos will win the day.

It is this sort of thinking that underlies much of mythic, analogical and metaphorical thinking, for, as Peterson says, this world of qualitative symbols infers an 'emergent property of first-order self-reference' and that it might be 'regarded as the interaction between the universe as subject and the universe as object' (1999: 290). This, of course, is exactly what the UFO exploits, for if one reads Jung or a large swathe of UFO literature, there is this constant paradoxical quality in which object becomes subject and vice versa. The 'cosmic viewpoint' is the realisation of *universe as subject*; in other words, it is implicit in our own being. After all, we constitute the universe by being inside it as much as, simultaneously, 'outside' it in the sense that we can become self-referential. To cease to be an outsider is to cease to be trapped in self-negation, and instead, finding a way out of the boundaries of personality and materialism towards a more elevated state of consciousness — and as a director of evolution.

On an individual level this can be seen with the individual versus mass-mindedness — or the Outsider and Western civilization — for it essentially equates to the same thing. Again,

Jung notes in *The Undiscovered Self* that just as the 'chaotic movements of the crowd, all ending in mutual frustration, are impelled in a definite direction by a dictatorial will, so the individual in his dissociated state needs a directing and ordering principle' (1990: 4). The individual, at odds with the immense unconscious forces of the world, must, in *himself*, experience — or know directly — something which is integrative of both inner and outer 'warring factions'. '[Ego-consciousness]... must *experience* them, or else it must possess a numinous *symbol* that expresses them and leads to their synthesis' (1990: 35). This, of course, was what Whitehead meant with his huge list of all existential experiences, and it is towards their integration that Jung, Wilson and the many other individuals we have discussed in this essay have pointed towards.

Each, in their own unique way, provides a model for the psyche's 'coming-to-terms' — through intuition and symbolism — with an evolutionary intentionality. The UFO will remain on the perimeter of this further discussion, but — suitable to its nature — it will return cloaked in a new order of logic which I will further explore in these proceeding sections.

Vast Active Imagination

It is impossible to study a system of the universe without studying man. At the same time it is impossible to study man without studying the universe. Man is an image of the world. He was created by the same laws which created the whole of the world. By knowing and understanding himself he will know and understand the whole world, all the laws that create and govern the world. And at the same time by studying the world and the laws that govern the world he will learn and understand the laws that govern him. In this connection some laws are understood and assimilated more easily by studying the objective world, while man can only understand other laws by studying himself. The study of the world and the study of man must therefore run in parallel, one helping the other.
–In Search of the Miraculous (2001: 75)

The above is quoted from *In Search of the Miraculous*, one of the most comprehensive books that systematises the teachings of GI Gurdjieff. However, it is clear in the context of this essay that it constitutes an evolutionary metaphor, particularly with its correlation between 'subjective' man and 'objective' universe and vice versa. Gurdjieff places heavy emphasis on the study of the *processes* of nature. These processes, he argues, are sufficient for gaining insights into the mechanisms of man; and, moreover, if properly understood, enables man to transcend their 'laws'. Gurdjieff's 'system' is based primarily on the notion that the man who truly knows the mechanisms of the cosmos is, in some sense, above them, for by understanding one—truly and not superficially—he can understand the other, that is *himself*. Furthermore he makes the important distinction between ordinary knowledge and *gnosis* (revelatory knowledge), or self-remembering. That is, rather than of simply knowing something mechanically, we *know* it in a deeper, more intimate sense—*we know more truly with all of its universal, objective and subjective correlates*. This gnosis is essentially Wilson's Faculty X, or what he called 'relationality'. We don't just passively glimpse 'other times and places'; we know that they are entirely real.

Interestingly there *are* symbols of wholeness, and this is precisely what the poet or artist—either consciously or unconsciously—is trying to achieve in his most visionary moments. There are also creative 'flashes' which enable someone to grasp wholes, which, once realised, relate to something else and so on until they constitute whole inner-landscapes of interrelated facts.

One of the most famous of visionary poems is 'Kubla Khan' by Samuel Taylor Coleridge which was, he says, composed 'in a sort of Reverie brought on by two grains of Opium' (1982: 12), in which he gained a vision—influenced from the night's reading—which constituted a *whole* poem. During a brief nap, he seems to have been a witness to the unconscious creative processes. '[T]he images rose up before him as *things* with a parallel production of the correspondent expressions, without any sensation or consciousness of effort' and upon awakening 'he appeared to himself to have a distinct recollection of the whole, and taking his pen, ink and paper, instantly and eagerly wrote down the lines' (1966 167). The conscious and unconscious processes are here blurred and intermixed: 'images rose up as *things*', these 'things' being manifestly perceptible. Also of interest is the fact that he was effectively unconscious, and beneath all this the 'dream artist' constructed its meanings in a type of logic usually unavailable to the conscious mind.

In this moment of integrative unconscious thinking working with the act of creativity, Coleridge was unfortunately interrupted by a trivial matter of business—this, it turned out, diminished the 'whole', breaking it into fragments of a vague and distant memory. Nevertheless, Coleridge, with acute phenomenological insight, managed to grasp the very process of the *loss* of this vision *and, significantly, its return*:

> ... all the charm
> Is broken—all that phantom-world so fair
> Vanishes, and a thousand circlets spread,
> And each mis-shape the other. Stay awhile,
> Poor youth! ...
> The stream will soon renew its smoothness, soon
> The visions will return! And lo, he stays,
> And soon the fragments dim of lovely forms
> Come trembling back, unite, and now once more
> The pool becomes a mirror. (1966: 167)

The 'thousand circlets', here, is the left brain's ordinary processing of time; its tendency to pixilation and to reduce things to 'bits'. Our perception of life is choppy like a fast, unpredictable disorder of associations, yet, in moments of insight the stream pools into a *reflective* insight; that is, as one looks into the pool, it reflects its environment back far more accurately. The left hemisphere's slowing down enables full images to be grasped by the right hemisphere—yet, significantly, it is in the stream of ordinary existence in which they are expressed, that is, in the form of something like Coleridge's poem.

Arthur Koestler remarked that the 'poet thinks both in images and verbal concepts, at the same time or in quick alternation; each *trouvaille*, each original find, bisociates two matrices. The dreamer floats among the phantom shapes of the hoary deep; the poet is a skin-diver with a breathing tube' (1966: 168). Certainly, Coleridge does seem to be in-between two states, and, once the harmonic was disturbed, he found himself more in one 'stream' of thought than the other. Temporarily he had slowed down his ceaseless perceptual 'firing'—by being drowsy and under the effects of opium—and had grasped an emergent and whole image from the unconscious mind. He then managed, albeit before the disruption, to capture fragments of the vision in the form poetry.

In *Mysteries* Colin Wilson cites the example of René Daumal's experiment with tetrachloride, which he used to inhale in order to descend into similar timeless and imaginal regions of the unconscious. In this state he suffered typical 'near death experiences' in which his whole life flashed before his eyes, and, eventually even words began to lose their meaning. Daumal entered 'an instantaneous and intense world of eternity, a concentrated flame of reality' in which he experienced a new type—or mode—of knowledge (342). In this state there was an odd play on words and sounds, with unusual incantations and 'formulas' which effected, or even *maintained*, various elements of Daumal's hallucinogenic visions. Ordinary words, by comparison, felt for Daumal too 'heavy and slow', 'shapeless' and 'rigid'. Daumal continues:

> With these wretched words I can put together only approximate statements, whereas my certainty is for me the archetype of precision. In my ordinary state of mind, all that remains thinkable and formulable of this experiment reduces to one affirmation on which I would stake my life: I feel the certainty of the existence of something else, a beyond, another world, or another form of knowledge.[17]

And yet, by contrast, *the words that sustained both his vision and his own existence*, Wilson remarks, are essentially a 'symbolic recognition that all life is sustained by a continuous act of will, or "intentionality".' As we have seen, this is Wilson's 'basic metaphysic' of a deep intentionality. It is an essential recognition that the force of life is in fact an extra-dimension of freedom consciousness—of the self-evolving kind—to enter the limited world of matter. Now, we may compare Coleridge's broken 'phantom-world' to one of Daumal's late poems:

I am dead because I have no desire,
I have no desire because I think I possess,
I think I possess because I do not try to give;
Trying to give, we see that we have nothing,
Seeing that we have nothing, we try to give ourselves,
Trying to give ourselves, we see that we *are* nothing,
Seeing that we are nothing, we desire to become,
Desiring to become, we live.
(2004: 119)

Each poem can be summarised by its initial loss of vision, its realisation of nothingness, but, in that 'loss', it aims to return to life—or, in Coleridge's terms, with a pool that becomes a mirror. At the heart of each there is a sense of affirmation, or what another poet Rainer Maria Rilke's called *'dennoch preisen'*—to praise *in spite* of. There is a limit, and once this is reached, felt existence, once again, returns to animate the very substratum of our being; our life and existence—intentionality, the primordial essence of being, underlies and animates a pure 'becoming', a stepping-up of complexification into ordinarily inanimate and unknowing forms. Gary Lachman refers to this as an 'inner "event horizon"'. He continues: '"I" seem to emerge like a fountain gushing out of a "nowhere" that is nonetheless within me. It is as if I reach a kind of horizon, beyond which I cannot see… Perhaps that inner "event horizon" there is a place where the unobservable mind and the unobservable universe meet?' (2013: 220).

A 'new knowledge' or gnosis comes into play on the other side of the perceptual event horizon, and, in an implicit sort of way it infers itself, rather like an evolutionary metaphor, through the dense, explicit nature of ordinary existence. Poets or people undergoing extreme and intense forms of consciousness are sometimes able to bring glimpses back, and, if they are capable enough, they create great pieces of art glistening with depths of meanings far beyond the artist's ordinary consciousness.

A descent into the unconscious makes one aware of the hidden machinery of our being, and indeed, our universe; we suddenly understand that just beneath the surface of existence is an animating force that works, in an odd way, on sound and manifestation—and, furthermore, it lies outside of time. It is, in fact, experienced and often described as if a part of a greater whole—this, of course, makes it difficult to articulate in a language unsuited to such conceptual enormity.

Now, Daumal realised that in spite of this feeling of wholeness and interconnectedness, he himself stood outside of it—he was, he felt, somehow a *distortion* in its patterning. One could say that one mind *is* in fact a distortion from this unconscious activity, for it is precisely *conscious of it*; one mind is a discontinuity between two modalities of being *and* phenomenon. Whereas the 'other' mind—the right brain—is a part of this 'other' world in as much as the 'spectator' is a part of its own (separate) world. Both 'I's' struggle to become aware of each other's existence simultaneously. And yet, there is a relation between the two worlds and one, without the other, would be a hollow and autonomous world and the other, by contrast, a vast chaos of formlessness and vacillation. Both Daumal's and Coleridge's visions reminded them of this fact—one world is 'nothing', whereas Coleridge's break from the 'phantom-world' is symbolised as an ever-increasing distortion of our vision: '... and a thousand circlets spread, / And each mis-shape the other.' But, significantly, Coleridge goes on to write, '... soon the fragments dim of lovely forms / Come trembling back'. This is the point in which the two worlds correspond, and the frontiers *cascade* into focus.

The essence of the living and the inanimate, the conscious and unconscious, is encapsulated in this extraordinary paragraph from van Vogt's 1948 short story, 'The Monster':

Out of the shadows of smallness, life grows. The level of

beginning and ending, of life and—not life; in that dim region matter oscillates easily between old and new habits. The habit of organic, or the habit of inorganic. Electrons do not have life and un-life values. Atoms know nothing of inanimateness. But when atoms form into molecules, there is a step in the process, one tiny step, that is of life—if life begins at all. One step, and then darkness. Or aliveness.

Van Vogt's 'monster', in fact, is a human being that has mastered the molecular level of his being, and once awakened by an extraterrestrial race on a post-apocalyptic Earth, becomes an unstoppable force of willpower and foresight. One single step awakens the man, and once this happens, he is an unstoppable spearhead of the life force.

Here the question arises: what is the essence and directive of being alive? If we blossom from some unseen dimension, then where is it we are emerging from? Once we have sketched out an approximate understanding of our own intentionality, and of our own inner world, we can begin to 'become' and live more *consciously*, and therefore freely. The stepping-up process of molecules into self-reflective, conscious beings that attempt to reach their own perceptual 'event horizons' tends to suggest that man thrives off an imagination that well exceeds our ordinary understanding of the evolutionary process. Man appears to want to embody the process himself—even steering it in accordance to his own will. Man, it is quite clear, is the ultimate intentional animal.

Now Carl Jung had the same vision of man when he arrived in Nairobi to visit the Athai Plains. Upon viewing the game reserve, he saw spread out before him a 'magnificent prospect' comprising to the limits of the horizon game animals like zebras, warthogs, antelopes etc., which were silent but for the 'melancholy cry of a bird of prey'. Reflecting upon it he felt that it was symbolic—and indeed, a literal vision—of 'the stillness of the eternal beginning, the world as it had always been, in the state of nonbeing' (1995: 284). Upon viewing nature as it is, he underwent a type of 'cosmic consciousness' in which the meaning of being became clear to him. Says Jung:

> Man, I, in an invisible act of creation put the stamp of perfection on the world by giving it objective existence. This act we usually ascribe to the Creator alone, without considering that in doing so we view life as a machine calculated down to the last detail, which, along with the human psyche, runs on senselessly, obeying foreknown and predetermined rules. In such a cheerless clock-world fantasy there is no drama of man, world, and God; there is no 'new day' leading to 'new shores', but only the dreariness of calculated processes. (1995: 284–285)

One part of man is essentially invisible — that which cannot be seen are precisely the meanings that are attributed to both himself and his environment, the exercise of his 'intentional self'. These meanings, of course, remain invisible *until they are expressed*; that is, until they are manifested into reality. When man works creatively, he brings forth this world in a dynamic between the invisible and the visible. Jung, in fact, quotes an alchemical dictum: 'What nature leaves imperfect, the art perfects.' Indeed, the world in which he lives is more vast and complex for man than any other creature — the world is, in its most fundamental sense, a grand mystery. In partaking in the unfolding of his own existence, and in his own awareness of life and death, man is truly in a state of 'in-between-ness'; between two worlds. Problems, such as psychological imbalance, existential angst, and so on, are essentially an issue of transmission between two modalities of perception — the problem between Whitehead's 'meaning perception' and Wilson's contrast between a worm's-eye view and a bird's-eye view of existence.

We return back to the 'cosmic viewpoint', that imperative of the UFO and, of course, science-fiction literature and esotericism. Both represent the polar opposite of the modern conception of the provinciality of man. The repositioning of metaphors, of worldviews and cosmological frameworks, furthermore, draws us onwards and upwards; it is, in essence, the invisible dynamo of the imagination and, therefore, our greatest asset in improving the transmission between two worlds and two minds. The evolutionary metaphor, in a sense, is the bridge that leads to a staircase—or a ladder—to the windowed attic of human super-consciousness.

The evolutionary metaphor is the working hypothesis that navigates implicit realities into explicit ones—the metaphor, being evolutionary, demands complexification as much as it requires control and discipline. For, without control, complexity becomes overwhelming, and this is the grave concern for Wilson's outsider. The world of increasing complexity collapses under its own weight, that is, unless it has a guiding metaphor that pulls it into an understandable shape—a comprehensive structure that *includes within itself a purposeful as well as dynamic future*. Effectively it is the symbolic cultural equivalent of the mandala of which Jung drew upon to represent the symbolic inner-unity of man's individual being.

In one of Terence McKenna's greatest speeches, he encapsulates what the outsider knows intuitively, and that is that '[man] was not put on this planet to toil in the mud', and referring to the mechanistic and materialistic culture as 'the machine' he argues that we express our own evolutionary directive more purposefully by living creatively. The evolutionary metaphor provides a vision in which we, as McKenna argues, 'maximize our humanness by becoming much more necessary and incomprehensible to the machine'—in inferring something beyond the limits of a pessimistic culture, it is, he demonstrates, a 'civil rights issue' in the sense that it is the suppression of the 'religious sensibility'. There is, in the language of this essay, an obfuscation of the invisible worlds of the imagination that are the very life's blood of consciousness and the evolutionary spirit.

Meanings always infer something more, and the more meaningful it is, the less constricting and narrow consciousness becomes. The evolutionary metaphor, insofar as it infers larger interdependent realities towards a larger and more inclusive whole, is fundamentally what Wilson meant by 'relationality'. To use one of Wilson's metaphors, ordinary consciousness is rather like a 'piano whose strings are damped so that each note vibrates for only a fraction of a second', but in our more 'wider' states:

> ... the strings go on vibrating and cause other strings to vibrate. One thing suddenly 'reminds' us of another, so the mind is suddenly seething with insights and impressions and ideas. Everything becomes 'connected'. We *see* that the world is self-evidently a bigger and more interesting place than we usually take for granted... We are simply in a state of wider perception—both outer and inner perception. (2008: 94)

As I have attempted to demonstrate throughout this essay, it is fundamentally this vision of consciousness, man and the cosmos, which may allow the enigma of the UFO to shed its secrets. If it is, as reliable theorists like Mack, Strieber and Kripal believe it to be—as an evolutionary 'wake-up' call of sorts— then it requires that we meet anomalous phenomenon halfway and recognise that fundamentally it is consciousness that can transcend the material limitations precisely by presaging a greater comprehension of existence itself—both inside and out.

A Convergence of Worlds

This essay sought to explore the possible esoteric, philosophical, and cosmological frameworks with which one could begin to understand the mystery of the UFO and its related phenomenon. In doing so, I decided to begin from the fundamental recognition at the heart of Wilson's new existentialism, that is: consciousness is intentional and can, in various situations, willed or unwilled, reach out and grasp the essential meanings that are implicit in existence.

The new existentialism acknowledges that there are levels of consciousness and that meaning, being the substratum as well as the evolutionary life force of existence itself, is relatively apprehended at each level. At higher levels we become aware of *increasing meaningfulness*; at lower levels we dis-integrate, and as a result, our sense of values decreases in proportion; eventually we cease to make any intentional effort required for the access of meaning. The latter becomes a vicious circle, whereas the former can achieve a level of 'positive feedback' by reinforcing itself after a certain level has been reached.

By examining the UFO mystery through the esoteric and phenomenological lenses provided by Wilson and others, what emerges is a symbol and metaphor for the development of a new paradigm in which human—and non-human—consciousness' role in evolution and reality is of crucial importance—and far exceeds its lowly position in our current materialistic climate. Wilson reached the same conclusion in *Alien Dawn*, for he sees both the UFO and occult phenomenon as forcing to us to accept a multidimensional understanding of reality. Indeed, he agrees with both Vallée and Mack, by considering the phenomenon to be heuristic in nature. '[S]omething,' Wilson writes, 'is trying to alter and widen our concept of reality' (1999: 372).

Later on in *Alien Dawn* Wilson discusses the meaning

of synchronicity, that is, as we may recall, of meaningful synchronous events—initially felt as an absurd coincidence—in which time and space are radically called into question. It is curious, at this point, to note the often symbolic and metaphoric nature of just *how* paranormal phenomenon provides for what Mack called an 'ontological shock'. The anomalous redefines our existential orientation, tilting it, as we shall see, towards a new paradigm—precisely a widened conception of reality.

The recognition of a level of deep intentionality as the underlying manifold of existence provides in itself a re-evaluation of what we call 'causal'; for if we accept the scientific materialist frame of reference there is only the cause and its inevitable effect. If we understand, like Michael Talbot, that consciousness is a 'reality-structurer' then what occurs regarding our present paradigm is a *'slow and continual change of axis from causality to synchronicity'* [my italics] (1991: 123). This recognition, which is of paradigmatic importance, suggests a new understanding on both existential as well as cosmological levels. The two, of course, reflect upon each other and are, moreover, interlinked. Now, if one accepts consciousness to be intentional, then, what is *relational* is what constellates the meaning in a web-like fashion; a bringing together of facts, of real meanings. The recognition, then, becomes that the world and consciousness are *synchronous* and fundamentally participatory in their revealing of meaning. In other words, consciousness is *the* essential part in bringing forth the implicit dimensions of reality; it is, above all, a reciprocal process. One could even call it nature's way of self-learning.

Wilson argues that these UFO entities whose 'powers far surpass our own nevertheless seem to be aiding us in our recognition of dimensions within ourselves which are equal to these entities.' He continues, '... from the point of view of the UFO entities, the human race is a species that is about to make the transition to a state that our visitors have already reached.'

Their purpose, he argues, 'is to help us make that transition.'

Now, if these entities are inter-dimensional and perhaps even cross over in some odd way with the dead—as Strieber has come to believe—how, then, do they get their messages across? How do they aid in this transition between two worlds, two perspectives? As I have tried to show throughout this essay, there is the important metaphorical element to much anomalous phenomena. Vallée even argues that the phenomenon is 'one of the ways through which an alien form of intelligence of incredible complexity is communicating with us symbolically'.

The science-fiction writer Philip K. Dick has also mentioned that when he saw the world with both hemispheres in synchrony *he experienced an entirely different world*. A world, we could say, experienced *synchronistically* rather than causally. To understand this phenomenon to its greatest extent, we need to begin to tilt our ontological axis so that the two worlds—perceptual and conceptual—converge. However, with the view of the abduction phenomenon this worldly transition doesn't come without its traumatic birth pangs. The work of John Mack and Budd Hopkins, along with the regression hypnotherapy records of many abductees, presents a daunting mountain of often terrifyingly icy impersonality and emotionless procedures of the medical variety.

And yet, despite this, many abductees discuss—after their integration of the trauma at the hands of competent psychiatrists, or through personal developments—a profoundly positive inner-change and deep recognition of another dimension of reality. Prior to this realisation, however, is a difficult adjustment period that challenges the individual—and sometimes whole families—on every level imaginable. Nevertheless, once a form of integration has taken place, and the abductee begins to understand his or her abduction in an entirely different light, then the experience itself becomes uniquely transformational.

What becomes of immense importance to the abductee

is the relationship between him- or herself and the trauma: there is, naturally, the initial sense of being a victim; one who is experimented upon and brutally examined without any permission or, indeed, any clearly defined reason. The abductee, as a result, is precisely traumatized by the sense of his/her utter powerlessness.

To understand this in a transformational framework it is worth applying what Jeffrey Kripal calls *the traumatic secret*, comprising a dialectic of the three components: *trauma, trance* and *transcendence*. Kripal begins from the same premise as Wilson, in that he too understands consciousness to be 'blinkered' when it comes to accessing larger dimensions of reality; it is, as Kripal rightly points out, precisely the 'human body-brain', the nervous system, which reduces consciousness in the same way that our laptop filters out many other signals and tunes into a specific bandwidth for its purposes. Otherwise, of course, the laptop, much like human consciousness, would be bombarded by a storm of chaotic, conflicting information which would send us spiralling into sensory overload. Kripal continues:

> Sometimes, however, the reducer is compromised or temporarily suppressed. The filtering or reduction of consciousness does not quite work, and other *forms of mind or dimensions of consciousness, perhaps even other species or forms of life, that are normally shut out now 'pop in'* [my italics].

If, as the phenomenon seems to hint, these entities exist in a state of matter—or form—which is dimensionally different from our own, then our consciousness too is in a state many dimensions parallel to ourselves; we access just a number of bandwidths out of a spectrum of consciousness, or conscious*nesses*. In other words, we too exist in one slither of a wide-ranging, inter-dimensional bandwidth, and what we experience as ourselves is only the reduced version of all that we are, *in potential*. Conversely this posits that the entities too can exist in realities entirely invisible to our own level of consciousness. Of course, this notion is altogether rejected by our current materialist paradigm, and this, in turn, generates a disorientating shift of perspective for the abductee whose fundamental existential axioms are severely compromised—resulting, indeed, in an 'ontological shock'.

The frustrating bridge for the abductee is the fact that they are experientially true events, and yet, both their logic forbids as well as, in some cases, the material, physical evidence. Often the abduction even seems to take place in their bedrooms, woods, or while driving their car; a UFO or bright light or orb appears in what is, essentially, the context of everyday existence, yet all the laws of time and space are broken. And, worst of all, they are usually left with only the traumatic experience to show for it, which is rejected as perhaps pathological and/or 'merely anecdotal'.

Let us briefly outline some common themes found in the abduction experience.

Once 'taken aboard' the craft, or vessel, or into another dimension entirely, the abductee often finds him- or herself in an utterly unfamiliar environment in which they are commonly, but not always, paralysed. Undergoing a battery of medical or surgical tests and procedures—another common feature—they are witness to an unusual entity, or group of entities, which are frequently described as insectoid-like, hairless, large-almond-eyed beings that often communicate in vague terms, usually via thought transference or telepathy. Again this is a general outline, for experiences vary largely in other cases, with descriptions in direct contrast to the 'common' traits and observances above.

Usually the event is followed by 'missing time' in which the abductee suddenly finds themselves an hour or more amiss (sometimes even days or weeks have been reported). In some cases they are clueless to the sequence of events leading up to the missing time period and simply have a 'blank'—or they have a general sense of unease, and 'flashbacks' of the events. These memories are often found buried, as it were, or repressed or removed altogether by a type of hypnotic suggestion. Retrieval of memory, in such circumstances, is often brought about either over time and happenstance, or the abductee undergoes hypnotherapy or psychiatric help to gain access to memories pertaining to the anomalous gaps of time. Or, indeed, they may emerge as symptoms such as irrational phobias, which, in themselves, suggest that they have undergone a deeply unusual experience of which they are not consciously aware.

These, for the sake of this essay, provide a general context from which to discuss the abduction experience, and it leads us on to discuss the transformational realities that result from these anomalous traumas.

One abductee, as detailed in Mack's *Abduction*, for the sake of anonymity called 'Eva', reports what she believes the role of abductions to be: 'To clean the body, physical body, in order for more information to come through' (1994: 260). Certainly this 'cleaning process' seems to be an incredibly traumatic experience. And yet, if our consciousness does indeed work as a reducing valve for other, larger and more potent realities, could the traumatic process be directly attributable to the process of this perceptual widening?

In *Miracle Visitors* Ian Watson observes a 'plus and minus factor at work' and this relates to the problem of injecting 'higher-order knowledge' for, in this process, 'something must change within the lower-order reality or be lost to it, to compensate.' He continues: 'The trick was to make the loss the least negative one possible—*to create merely mystery, not damage*' [my italics]. Mystery, of course, is best served symbolically, thus preserving the *implicit* content of the message in such a way that after careful consideration and integration *the meaning reveals itself equal to the interpreter's level of consciousness*. Other than that, one could simply open all of the doors of perception at once, as it were.

A sudden revealing of this whole new reality would, perhaps, overwhelm the reducing mechanism, causing irreparable psychic damage. Metaphoric expression, therefore, becomes a sort of 'stepping-down' process, and the most painless means to widen our perceptual range.

Now 'Eva', like Kripal, goes on to mention that it is the physical body—the nervous system—that is being cleansed. Trauma, of course, often has a deeply physical component, and many of the procedures undergone in the abduction experience do appear to relate directly to the body, and yet it is difficult to discern *which body* they are operating upon. It seems, at times, to be both/and the physical body and what we might call a 'spirit' or non-physical body. The 'body', in fact, may be a metaphorical representation of our consciousness as it is disembodied from the physical—that is, it composes a sort of 'mental body', symbolically or actual.

Curiously another abductee, 'Carlos', in Mack's chapter 'A Being of Light', describes leaving his body and floating through walls and windows—all solid materiality seemed to be no obstacle. 'Carlos' also describes the 'transubstantial bodily-material changes' in which he 'dissolves' at a cellular level through a painful process of 'breaking from material form into light energy' (1994: 343). Again here two or more realities are blurred and a third state is suggested: an existence in which, apparently conscious, we are subsumed or transubstantiated into a vast manifold of light. The religious connotations, of course, are clear if we think of Catholicism and the transubstantiation of the body of Christ. This state of being is often referred to as simultaneously a state of after (physical) life and, indeed, as a stage *before* we inhabit corporeal existence as a physical body. 'Carlos' describes the location of this light-realm as simply, 'out of space. It was not space/time' (1994: 343). This will become increasingly important as we discuss the work of the psychologist Stanislav Grof.

Before we move on it is worth turning to another description of a reality in which the laws of consensual reality, and our understanding of human consciousness, are dramatically turned inside out. This case, however, concerns an individual who has had no such experience with UFO entities, but instead experimented with his own consciousness. It concerns the Russian philosopher, already mentioned in this essay, Ouspensky, who describes his extraordinary experiences in an essay entitled, 'Experimental Mysticism', in his book *A New Model of the Universe*. It is likely that these experiments were conducted with the aid of nitrous oxide (dental gas).

Ouspensky warns us that such experiences of these intense states are influenced, more generally, by the philosophical or religious context, or interpretative language, through which the experiencee is enmeshed. Each framework or point-of-view presupposes its own epistemology which, in turn, attempts to approach the phenomenal and numinous experiences within its own structure. And each experience, rather like that of 'Carlos', will be tainted with words, concepts and terminologies which remind one of another belief system. These are, effectively, the paradigms in which one operates, but, nevertheless, they do share a common experience *of something numinous*, unexplainable, and baffling to ordinary language. They are, says Ouspensky, at best approximations of another reality.

Ouspensky describes his own experience in which the 'objective and subjective could change places', and 'the habitual mistrust of the subjective disappeared; every thought, every feeling, every image, was immediately objectified in real substantial forms which differed in no way from the forms of objective phenomenon' (1989: 314). In this state, we may venture, the subjective nature of an evolutionary metaphor, then, might become a reality in itself; and which, on the other side of the dimensional partition, so to speak, it once again becomes a symbol, or, as Ouspensky calls it, a 'motif'. A 'motif', for him, became a relational pattern which was represented as a 'very complicated design' developing out of a set of simple laws. And yet, it had a recursive, highly information-rich nature which could suddenly switch between various modes of expression and manifestation: music, a visible form, a sort of mosaic design, which in turn could be turned again, back into sounds, music and any other apparently unique modality of expression. All this took place, he says, in a dimension of 'mathematical laws' (1989: 315).

Language too took on this complex self-referential quality. So much so in fact he could proceed no further than uttering the simple phrase 'I said yesterday...' before yielding to its sheer implications, its interrelated complexity and meaning-content that was associated with each of the three words. Identity: communication: time. A sense of an infinity of relations opened up before him with each utterance. 'I', for example, unravelled philosophical as well as psychological realities regarding the nature of identity. The word 'said' produced further ideas related to 'speech, the possibility of expressing thoughts in words, the past tense of the verb', and each of these 'ideas produced an explosion of thoughts, conjectures, comparisons and associations' (1989: 316).

'Experimental Mysticism' provides a brief glimpse into an extraordinary richness relating to even the most apparently ordinary realities we take for granted. Everything, it seemed for Ouspensky, took on an almost infinitely *relational* quality, to the point that even a trivial object such as an ashtray could send him into a vision of endless documentary of origin—design and conception, from the trivial, everyday practical manufacturing of the object to its cosmic significance and origin.

An important point, however, is that Ouspensky was no passive or neutral observer of these visions, rather they involved an enormous emotional component in which feelings of 'joy, wonder, rapture, horror' continually changed 'into one another' and would often correspond with the vast unfolding spectacle before him. Although trauma may be too strong a word to use for Ouspensky's visionary experience, this does not prevent us from drawing a parallel with the transformational knowledge attested to by so many abductees, who similarly undergo an experiential spectrum of emotion and emerge with an ability, to adopt Ouspensky's phrase, to 'think in other categories' (paradigms).

In fact, Ouspensky recorded his insight and found, when he became sober, that he had written down the phrase 'think in other categories'; a curious message that has much in common with alien abduction literature. Indeed, it provides an explanation for some of the more symbolic claims of the entities in which visions, usually presented on a screen or inside the abductees' minds as an inner-panorama, forewarn the human race about their future. Many of these sometimes dire visions seem to be intended to be interpreted somewhere between a metaphor and a reality, and the urgency for change more often than not refers directly to human consciousness. Mack importantly highlights the allegorical nature of much of the content, suggesting that, reminiscent of Ouspensky's experience described above, 'the realms of consciousness and of existence to which abductees travel during their experiences *the distinction between the literal and the metaphoric or the objective and the subjective, seems to lose its power*' [my italics] (1994: 109). Amusingly one bewildered abductee, 'Ed', even protested, asking the entities: 'Why do you talk to me in allegory? I'm no poet!'

The Swiss artist and occultist, Oswald Wirth, has written about the apparently infinite, analogical quality of symbolism in *Le symbolisme hermétique:*

A symbol can always be studied from an infinite number of points of view; *and each thinker has the right to discover in the symbol a new meaning corresponding to the logic of his own conceptions.*

As a matter of fact symbols are precisely intended to awaken ideas sleeping in our consciousness. They arouse a thought by means of suggestion and thus cause the truth which lies hidden in the depths of our spirit to reveal itself [my italics]. (1989: 217)

If, of course, there are dimensional similarities between the UFO entities and Ouspensky's access into a world of 'mathematical laws', a world in which our categories are switched inside out, and where objective and subjective are reversed, then we might expect some interesting correspondences between the two. Wirth places emphasis on the unconscious or subconscious significance of symbols in their quality for unveiling hidden dimensions ordinarily obscured from the conscious mind. Indeed, Gary Lachman calls this 'knowledge of the imagination'. He continues: 'Imagination has a noetic character; it is the source and medium of our other way of knowing' (2017: 31). Another abductee, Paul Roberts, uses similar language, however, the importance of light, like with the case of 'Carlos', is once again present. Roberts describes these entities as being 'made of thought and light. *They were ideas—but real ideas—and what they brought and still bring is a super-condensed form of truth'* [my italics].

Now none of this reality seems to be 'contained' in the unconscious mind, rather that *the unconscious mind has access beyond the reducing valve of ordinary consciousness.* The post-Jungian James Hillman differentiates himself from Jung's concept of the unconscious for the same reason, for the unconscious, as Harpur describes, is 'not located "inside us", nor is it a "container" of archetypal images. It is not, in other words, a literal "place" at all, but *a metaphor, a tool for deepening and interiorizing experience,* a representation of the soul's richness, depth and complexity' (2003: 120). It is the point of convergence between two worlds and not a discontinuity, a mere islet limited to its own relatively meagre resources—indeed, the unconscious is an open system rather than a closed one. Jung himself expresses a similar idea to an open-system unconscious mind. One might, for our purposes, replace 'myth' with 'metaphor' or 'symbol' in the quote below:

> Only here, in life on earth, where the opposites clash together, can the general level of consciousness be raised. That seems to be man's metaphysical task—which he cannot accomplish without 'mythologizing'. Myth is the natural and indispensable intermediate stage between unconscious and conscious cognition. (1995: 343)

The unconscious, Jung continues, has—in contrast to ordinary consciousness' linear and time-bound knowledge—'knowledge' that is 'without reference to the here and now, not couched in language of the intellect' (1995: 343). (Again, reminiscent of Ouspensky's experiment and Lachman's 'knowledge of the imagination'.) It is, in essence, Wilson's recognition of a life force which, through intentionality and relationality, reaches beyond space and time into a vital, effervescent upsurge of peak experience and Faculty X—a sense of other times and places. It is also what Ian Watson meant by 'UFO wisdom': 'an awareness of the universe thinking itself, creating itself, evolving itself.' Again it is the meeting point of two worlds that grow *through* each other in a creative, participatory, dialectical involution-evolution.

Maurice Nicoll, another Jungian, in his wonderful book, *Living Time and the Integration of the Life*, also uses the words 'two worlds': 'The soul stands between the sensible world and the world of Ideas—between two orders of "reality"' and when an individual has attained synchronous existence along with a causal one he 'sees clearly—with increasing clearness—because he has become a meeting-point of two worlds, one reached within and through himself, and the other reached without, and through his senses' (1976: 37). Evolutionary metaphors, here, become bridges into the *real*.

In one of Wilson's now little-read books, *Strange Powers* (1973), he coins a term for this sort of experience—'bridge period'. It also returns us nicely back to Kripal's *traumatic secret* and its transformational, ontological shock which initiates a new stage in an individual's consciousness. Wilson describes the 'bridge period':

> During these periods, you sense that something is happening, some basic change, of the sort that occurs at puberty. But then, when the body changes at puberty, you are aware that this is a purely subjective change; it is happening to you, not to the rest of the world. But in other bridge periods, there is *a curious feeling that can only be described as 'involvement', as if you are involved in some wider, more general change* [my italics]. (1973: 112)

Wilson's 'bridge period' appears to be closely related to the experience of what we might call 'a synchronous life'—when a deep sense of meaningfulness seems to underlie our existence, our actions. Indeed, Wilson himself experienced such a 'bridge period' in the form of synchronicities while writing *Alien Dawn*, for he mentions a curious occurrence in which, while working through the problem of UFOs, he was regularly seeing an arrangement of three-digits consisting of the same numbers on his digital alarm clock: 1:11, 2:22, 3:33, 4:44, and so on. In his analysis of the phenomenon he expresses a similar sense of a 'bridging' between two worlds: causal and synchronous. The latter is a finer world in which, as we have seen, meanings, ideas, symbols and the power of the mind and consciousness are far more fluid, and far less restricted to laws than the physical, material world. Like Jung said, we are somewhere in-between and synchronicity, myth and evolutionary metaphors can only be played out in a symbolic form for our Earthly existence.

Kripal's *traumatic secret* and its transformational potentialities can be best tested on Earth. In his autobiography, *Dreaming to Some Purpose*, Wilson acknowledges that 'being alive is grimly hard work', yet, in states of what he calls 'duo-consciousness' we are *'in two places at once'*, and this other 'mind' is the cause of synchronicities. The 'bridge-period', sometimes traumatic and jarring, is nevertheless our first foretaste, perhaps, of a whole new world—alien or otherwise.

Indeed, UFO entities, Wilson concludes in *Alien Dawn*, seem to have 'no such problems with solid matter' and, he continues, 'we would be the same if we had reached their level of evolution.' They have, in some sense, bridged the gap between two worlds for themselves, and they may be, in their own enigmatic way, encouraging our own *self-determined* leap into a higher level of consciousness.

We shall now look at other examples of trauma to transformational states, but this time in examples of worldly shamanic traditions.

Shamanism: Walking Between Worlds

The more one reads and is receptive towards the subtleties found in the literature and witness testimonies regarding the UFO phenomenon, one feels, quite distinctly, that there is a strange merging of two worlds, one overlapping the other. Moreover, they seem to be oddly complementary, one in urgent *need* of the other's existence.

Now, of course, there is a rather disquieting element to all this, for there is a persistent theme throughout concerning an inter-species breeding program in which there is, in some cases, biological material such as sperm and eggs extracted from the bodies of abductees. However, it is not entirely clear how precisely this is a *real event*, for the evidence of physical traces such as phantom pregnancies and so on are remarkably rare considering the relatively wide selection of abductees who have come forward. Indeed, many of the cases that *do* exhibit physical signs and symptoms may be explained as placebo effect; rather like the many instances of the stigmata phenomenon with religious devotees. Yet UFOs themselves also seem to be able to switch between dimensions, material and non-physical, while popping in and out. Sometimes they're even detected by radar.

It is now worth considering shamanism which, as its practitioners often claim, directly concerns individuals, initiated shamans, who are able to walk between worlds; and again, the notions of subjective and objective are blurred. There is also the famous 'shaman's illness' which involves all of the familiar elements of both trauma and transformation as described above. Patrick Harpur describes the shaman's ordeal:

... sudden illnesses, fits or fainting spells; a 'big dream'; or, above all, an unexpected state of trance or ecstasy. While in this state, the recipient undergoes a visionary experience whose contents invariably include one or more of the following features: a dismemberment of the body by 'spirits' (daimons) or by the souls of dead shamans; a purging or scraping down of the body which is then reconstructed with new organs of 'iron bones'; an ascent to the sky, followed by a dialogue with gods or spirits; a descent to the Underworld, followed by conversation with subterranean spirits and the souls of dead shamans. (2003: 232)

Aside from the physical element of sickness, bodily or psychological with each of its related illnesses, ecstatic trances and so on, all of the later instances of the shamanic ordeal as outlined by Harpur are seemingly undertaken in another world or dimension. Here the shaman—like the abductee—undergoes a rigorous form of spiritual and physical purging. We may here recall 'Eva' who said that the purpose of abduction is to adjust the physical body and its nervous system, to expand our access to other levels of consciousness and reality. This too, it becomes apparent, is the purpose of the bodily adjustments as undergone by the shaman, and, moreover, the shamanic testimony and history provides a general universality of agreement across cultures.

In *Sky Shamans of Mongolia*, for example, Kevin Turner shares a brief interview with a Buryat master shaman called Bair Rinchinov who, at the ceremony of an initiation of other potential shamans who are ascending—*both* physically and mentally—a sort of Great World Tree, describes his own *shanar* (initiation): 'I became very frightened and thought I was dying. I had the feeling that my soul flew out. I saw the whole region, the local area below me, as if I were flying in a very vast plane' (2016: 146). One is here again reminded of the notion that consciousness can exist outside of the body and the experience, as is often reported, is traumatic and accompanied by a general loss of control. In short one could say that in light of the shamanic tradition the abduction phenomenon also, in its own unique way, represents the Western form of 'initiatory illness'.

The shamanic tradition, fortunately, has a unique *context in which they can deal with these incursions from another reality,* and they are able to shift, with more conscious deliberation, from the state of trauma to transformation due, simply, to being able to identify and diagnose the 'illness' correctly and early on.

Shamanism has a very complex history, and it would not benefit the purposes of this essay to describe it at great length. However, it is here worth mentioning the components of which they, abductees and shamans, share. Again we can see crossovers which highlight the similarities between the shaman's dealings with the inter-world and the abductee/UFO phenomenon.

A shaman of the Diné tradition and a part of the Navajo Nation, located in the south-west of the United States and stretching from the north-east of Arizona through to Utah and New Mexico, Walking Thunder—a name given to her by her community—is an authority on the traditional medicines of her people. Although the medicines are herbal in nature, many of her reports cover similar ground as reported in *Sky Shamans of Mongolia*. Again we see a wide range of correspondences between cultures which are separated by thousands of miles of land and sea. Walking Thunder also produces sand paintings, usually a symbolic image acquired or visualised by the shaman, often in a dream, and is then used as a sort of charm or blessing which heals or encourages the growth of a particular dimension of their patients' lives.

Originally somewhat sceptical about the shamanic practice in her culture she one day ransacked and broke a number of sacred objects which, for her community and its medicine man alike, were deeply significant and powerfully charged. One object in particular, a doll which she understood as 'a holy person', became the figure of her attention, and to test the realities of their deeply-held beliefs she decided to go ahead and break the doll in half. The medicine man, presumably distraught and furious, warned her, '... something is going to happen to you.' Walking Thunder was cynical, basically disbelieving him, and shouted in defiance that she thought no such thing would come of the event. And yet, in a few weeks, she became severely sick, apparently both physically and psychologically. As a result she became a misfit in the community. 'I was told that I was sick, handicapped, retarded and crazy. Everyone rejected me' (2008: 19).

Her mother, no doubt upset with her daughter's increasingly irrational behaviour and resulting social stigma, took her to something called a 'Talking Back Ceremony', which is remarkably similar to regression hypnotherapy undergone by many abductees. It demands, she says, that 'you examine your past and talk back to it' (19). During the ceremony she was dressed as a 'bear symbol' and surrounded by herbs. The medicine man began to whistle until she 'felt a wound opening on top of my head.' She continues: 'I felt him take something out of my head with his mouth. He growled, pulled it out, and spit it into the fire.' After this she was told she would be able to begin to see into the future. Time, for her, would be experienced in a fundamentally different way.

As a becoming medicine woman her senses, particularly olfactory, became so sensitive she claimed she could both see and 'smell sickness', although, at first, this was almost overwhelming and intolerably out of control. To 'retune' and heal her mind she was administered the hallucinogenic cactus, *peyote*, which 'fixed me up inside and my body hurt from it,' and after that her *'vision focused like a TV set and I could see into my past'* [my italics] (35). Adjusting to her new powers she became a recognised shamanic healer among her community and apparently acquired miraculous powers; one of which was an ability to leave her bodily perception and view the position and circumstances of people deemed missing. This ability she called 'crystal vision'—a typical type of out-of-body state.

Walking Thunder's testimony has all of the familiar elements as discussed in regards to the abduction experience: illness, trauma, transformation and oddly symbolic 'objects' placed in and extracted from her body. And, finally, the radical shift in consciousness which facilitates the emergence of paranormal abilities; a novel adjustment to reality and time, and a controlled sense of leaving her body.

It is interesting to note that Walking Thunder also perceived bright lights in and around people at crucial moments in their lives; particularly prior to a death of some close relative. She mentions that her husband David, also a healer, 'saw a bright red-orange light outside our window' (33). She, too, reported seeing a red-orange light at 'eleven o'clock one night to go out to work. When I started the car, everything went bright red-orange around the area.' Although, unlike UFO phenomena, this, for both witnesses, is an experience associated with death. And yet, what is the nature of the light itself, and *why* does it signify death? Is the light, in some sense, a form of disembodied consciousness, a soul perhaps, or indeed is it, in fact, somehow related to the UFO phenomenon?

In *Abduction* Mack notes that the abductee 'Jerry' woke up one November night in 1991 to see, again like David and Walking Thunder, 'an orange-red light'; this experience, however, is not directly related to death, but instead her mind was, as she described it, 'turned up full volume' and flooded with information of a 'universal' quality. This was expressed in an unusual flurry of poetry and prose, which according to 'Jerry' was most unlike her. These poems and writings that were somehow 'initiated' by the orange-red light do, like Walking Thunder, relate to death, although many other topics and themes were also meditated upon. Mack, who viewed these writings, said that they were concerning 'a vast range of existential matters, including the nature of time, space, and the universe itself; the great cycles of birth, death and creation; the mysteries of truth, spirit and soul; and the limitations of material science' (140). One wonders if 'Jerry', within Walking Thunder's tradition, would too become a recognised shaman?

'Jerry' called her 'force' an archetypal creative principle of the universe; Walking Thunder's sand paintings were dictated by dreams, and her guiding force, as she refers to it, is simply called the 'Creator', for whom the eagle is an archetypal symbol, or 'life line to the Creator' (43). The similarities are clear, but what seems to most commonly bind them together is the recognition of a deep, creative force that can be experienced symbolically and metaphorically. There is, it seems, a cosmology of deep intentionality.

In his later book, *Passport to the Cosmos: Human Transformation and Alien Encounters*, John Mack notes that in the wake of his controversial *Abduction* he: 'began to be contacted by medicine men and other native leaders... who were familiar in their own societies with what I had been finding out about the alien abduction phenomenon.' Shamans from around the world, it turned out, had their own unique experiences and vocabulary for meetings with these entities. Conversely, many Western abductees were turning to the wisdom of the native and shamanic beliefs in the understanding that these ancient practices have the interpretive as well as therapeutic methods for integrating the phenomenon with both its traumatic and spiritual elements.

It is here worth looking at the case of Vusamazulu Credo Mutwa, a South African *sangoma* (shaman), and the spiritual leader of the Zulu *sangomas* and *sanusis* (a combination of clairvoyant and a keeper of knowledge). Being one of the most famous healers of his kind he is also an historian as well as an author in his own right. Upon meeting him Mack noted that his 'understanding of African spirituality and culture is astounding, and he knows that contained within this great body of knowledge there are truths that can benefit humankind in our time of crisis'

(199).

Mutwa's initial 'shaman's illness' occurred after the very this-worldly experience of being raped by mineworkers in 1937 at the age of sixteen. Becoming increasingly ill and feverish as a result, this experience nearly proved fatal. Like many abductees and shamans this trauma resulted in a form of inner-transformation, and a heightened degree of extrasensory powers like mindreading and the perceiving of 'auras' of those around him. It was his grandfather, Ziko Shezi, another *sangoma*—whom Credo's Roman Catholic father 'despised as a heathen and demon worshiper'—who in fact brought him back to health through traditional African practices. His grandfather identified the illness as a typical 'sacred illness which required that [Credo Mutwa] had to become a shaman, a healer.' The trauma to transformation process required, in Mutwa's case, little supernatural agency, for the trauma was brutally terrestrial in origin.

Turning to a 'heathen' belief system that was considered not only heretical but also demonic, Mutwa found himself somewhat an outsider. His spiritual as well as personal development mirrors that of Walking Thunder's initial social ostracization. After travelling extensively 'for knowledge, in search of clarity of mind and in search of the truth about my people,' he found to some degree of satisfaction his life's purpose. A brave and noble one, it consisted of the daunting task, as Louis Proud describes, 'to help preserve the culture of his people, and to help mend the problems in his country, of drugs, unemployment, crime, disease and poverty.' It was, however, Proud continues, Mutwa's belief that much of 'humanity's difficulties can be explained by the negative influence of manipulative extraterrestrial beings'— particularly from whom he calls the *mantidane*.

Mutwa's uniquely anomalous form of trauma reportedly happened in 1958 when he was out collecting medicinal herbs in the sacred Inyangani Mountains of Rhodesia. Suddenly, he recalls, the familiar sounds of birdsong and the rustling of gently windblown trees was replaced by a 'strange silence' which 'lasted only a few moments'. This was followed by the occurrence of an obscuring blue mist that seemed to envelop the landscape. Without apparently any transition Mutwa suddenly found himself in what he describes as 'a place made of iron' which was 'round, like a tank, a water tank lying on its side' (210). A common description of the interior of a UFO. Becoming aware of shiny and oily doll-like beings, which appeared to move in a staggering and awkward manner, there was one which stood out as distinctly female.

This feminine entity appeared cold and procedural, and she proceeded to insert some unidentifiable instrument into both his thigh and his head. He describes the experience as 'a terrible witchcraft'. While undergoing a rather austere and passionless form of sexual intercourse with this female entity, which seemed to him oddly boneless, he appears to have been used as a part of a now familiar 'breeding program'. Indeed, he was even shown a fetus of an unborn baby suspended in pinkish liquid contained in an apparently glass bottle. This traumatic experience, with many familiar elements of a typical UFO abduction case, he again attributes to the *mantidane*.

Both Mutwa's brief biographical account and his related experiences present a challenging case, for it combines both an insight into the shamanic experience, as well as an essentially negative and brutal abduction experience. Another difficulty is extracting Mutwa's own influence upon and interpretation of (recall Kripal's 'making the cut') the phenomenon itself, for his difficult and traumatic background may indeed generate or bias the content of his experience. Furthermore, his claims of the experience granting him extraordinary powers and an apparently miraculous access to new forms of knowledge makes the case very difficult to disentangle. There is, of course, also the problem of distinguishing between the mythological and traditional interpretations of his people, particularly in regards to its lineage of folklore which owe its longevity to a long-lasting oral tradition.

Nevertheless, Mutwa's consistency with the themes and experiences of Western abductees is also too present in his testimony to ignore. And with such unusual and potentially universal reports of a similar nature, it would be unwise to dismiss what this impressive high *sanusi* and *sangoma* has to say.

One emerges from Mutwa's account with a sense of gloomy fatality. The *mantidane* appear to be infinitely superior beings which are essentially driven by nothing more than selfish, cold survival, with little respect or warmth, at least on any deep level, of humankind. And yet, paradoxically, Mutwa shares his own experiences in which he accesses degrees of almost superhuman states of consciousness which seems to infer that we, mankind, may not be so fatally destined after all.

There are two such examples. The first concerns his sensation of something bursting 'from the small of your back' during an ecstatic initiatory dance. This force, he continues, rises up through your spine and bursts forth through the top of one's head and 'explodes into space and seems to float towards the stars' (126). One is, Mutwa describes, overcome by the force of the 'hidden one', 'the *ncumu*' in which a sensation of leaving your body is achieved and one enters a state of blissful 'eternal peace' in which consciousness is felt to be universalized, expanded to incorporate, experientially, all of creation. Elsewhere, he describes his belief that 'the human mind is capable, under certain intensely emotional circumstances, of achieving what one might call the impossible' (137). This, the reader may recall, bears some resemblance to Ouspensky's account of his emotionally-charged experiences under nitrous oxide.

Mutwa even goes on to suggest that our minds can not only influence reality, but can also *create* thought-forms, a kind of *tulpa*, in which we can 'create ghost figures that other people, no matter how skeptical, can perceive' (137). Individuals, who gather together, he claims, can also form one single mind—so, one wonders, what sort of realities, or thought-forms, might perhaps emerge from a collective mind, all focusing upon a singular purpose?

A second example takes place after a sacred dance in which he knelt before his teacher, Felapakati, and experienced what could be described as a peak experience. With almost mystical intensity, which, again, consisted of a 'strange explosion inside my head', Mutwa describes the sensation consisting of a 'silver fog', followed by 'a strange and totally inexplicable burst of joy' (126). The now familiar state of the universal consciousness once again flooded him, and he could hear millions of voices of people apparently from afar—both of the dead and the living...

In concluding his brief biographical account and exploration of his beliefs, he shares a symbol of cosmic death and rebirth, in which the whole universe, in its final stages, 'recalls each fugitive galaxy and runaway star, when the planets are once more called to become one with the great mass where a new universe will be born... in the eternal dark, until the voice of God is heard again, and creation is reborn' (143).

It is, perhaps, this poetic cosmology, consisting of vast scales of death and rebirth, which is reflected in the individual's transition from trauma to transformation. For, as Mack says, it is this resulting 'psychic chaos [of trauma that] is a metaphor for the precosmogenic chaos' out of which a new universe—or consciousness—is reborn. Possibly, at some crucial juncture in our *social existence*—in which the Western hemisphere with its constricting materialism is incurred upon by entities from beyond. Entities that nurture the birth process of a new potentially transformational paradigm. And thus, in themselves and through their actions, provide us with evolutionary metaphors for a new age.

Another Way Outside—A Cosmic Conclusion?

[T]he lurid character of so many of these contacts prevents them from being taken seriously by the scientific establishment of the target society, and instead these experiences are allowed to sink into the deeper, dreamlike psychical substrate that defines the mythic folklore of that culture.

–Jason Reza Jorjani, *Prometheus and Atlas*

In this final section it is not my intention so much to conclude but as to expand the question; to widen our field of enquiry in the hope that, by examining paradigms, we may evolve our metaphors and our conceptual frameworks. With such a field as ufology it would, of course, be absurd to make premature conclusions. One can at least hope to provide a philosophical context which can absorb some of its more challenging contents. This, as we shall see, opens up many new pathways towards a more general understanding of the phenomenon and ourselves.

Paradigms are in themselves models, which, when they become incompatible with reality—or with a new and prevailing paradigm—are often painfully, sometimes bloodily, discarded as a new shift takes place. 'A paradigm shift,' Jason Reza Jorjani explains in *Prometheus and Atlas*, 'is a change in worldview that occurs when anomalies pile up and lead to a crisis wherein competing factions fight for different new paradigms' (2016: 4). These shifts are rarely rational, Jorjani concludes, for each contending paradigm has differing standards of evaluation.

Simply, then, this final section will aim to understand the birth of paradigms as they might occur if, that is, the evidence and speculations availed from ufology is to be integrated into a newly emerging worldview.

If we combine what we have explored so far—each with its

unique set of implications—we may create a 'creative resonance'[18] from which we can gestalt a new evolutionary model. In doing so, we may gain an interpretative lens through which we can glimpse a Wilsonian 'bird's-eye view' of the phenomena.

The subtitle of a recent book by Thomas Sheridan, *Sorcery* (2018), is 'The Invocation of Strangeness'. And if anything this essay has been precisely an attempt to do just that. After all, the enjoyment found in creativity and unusual juxtapositions is precisely because of their newness, their exciting perspective that reminds us that the world is a wondrous and mysterious place full of implicit potentialities awaiting actualisation. Our consciousness, as we have seen, is precisely buoyed up by symbols, and it is precisely this intensity of the intentional apprehension of symbolic realities that reveals their *inner* nature, Lachman's 'knowledge of the imagination'.

Maurice Nicoll, for example, warns us against becoming 'sunk in appearances' for we quickly become dead 'through lack of realisation of the mystery of the world' (1976: 216). 'We are dead,' Nicoll continues, 'because we do not try to understand, because we never face the mystery of existence with any real thoughts of our own, because we are satisfied with explanations which prevent us from beginning to think' (216). The symbolic and metaphoric offers us an intuitive means with which to acknowledge the mysteries of the inner world, for here, clearly, nothing is as it seems. It wasn't a random act of hyperbole that Jeffrey Kripal began *The Super Natural* with the warning of an 'apocalypse of thought' waiting the reader's actualisation; for it *is* very much about a new world being recognised. Indeed, the birth pangs of a whole mysterious universe are at stake.

In his book on cosmology and astronomy, *Starseekers*, Wilson notes how the left hemisphere of the brain proceeds logically, step-by-step, and 'operates by imposing a rational structure on the world, which has the effect of "familiarizing" the environment'

(1980: 26). It is a crucially important survival mechanism which, in imposing 'a kind of gigantic grid on the world', provides a degree of control over what would be, without rationality, logic and an understanding of quantity, a certain doom for our species. We'd be adrift in chaos without all of the benefits of prediction that comes with familiarization. For this we have the 'robotic' part of ourselves to thank, for it provides order and control over chaos and results in the uncountable benefits of modern civilization.

And yet, Wilson continues, 'the idea of the infinity of space makes it dizzy, while it doesn't seem to bother the right brain— our "intuitive self"—in the least' (1980: 26). This, of course, applies to any anomalous phenomenon for it frustrates and challenges familiarity by introducing the unpredictable, the strange, and denies the 'grids'—paradigms—with which our whole left brain relies. In contrast, the anomalous, for the right brain, is quite energizing and interesting, it reconnects us to *a healthy balance of wonderment equal to the familiar*; a dynamic interaction between the two. In Coleridge's words it: 'excite[s] a feeling analogous to the supernatural, by awakening the mind's attention from the lethargy of custom, and directing it to the loveliness and the wonders of the world before us; an inexhaustive treasure' (2012: 173). It benefits a type of novelty which reconnects us with our inner world, rather than, that is, a jarring or shocking form of 'newness' that is symptomatic of the disconnected, essentially nihilistic, postmodern worldview... '[T]o create merely mystery not damage', as Watson said in *Miracle Visitors*.

Many of the UFO experiences have, of course, many elements of shock and forcefulness, but once these are correctly integrated they become, as we have seen, a deeply enriching and integrating phenomenon. Wilson argues, however, that a more 'positive intervention would be self-defeating, since the aim is to persuade human beings to take the crucial step themselves' (1999: 337).

In attempting to make sense of the phenomenon one is forced

to creatively re-contextualise—to alter our understanding of various deeply entrenched beliefs and laws—for the phenomenon simply cannot be explained, to any degree of satisfaction, by materialist science or even conventional logic. Many writers, including Wilson, conclude their books on the phenomenon with recourse to the equally baffling, but no less insightful, world of contemporary research into quantum physics. Reality, cause and effect, and so on, in these subatomic worlds, obey radically strange and novel laws.

Similarly this is also reflected in books on evolution itself, for in his book *Evolutionaries* (2012), Carter Phipps concludes that, 'Over time, our understanding of the evolutionary process trends towards theories of development that involve more creativity and agency and that are less deterministic' (349). Increasingly modern science is becoming 'well schooled in the indeterminacies of quantum physics and the unpredictable self-organizing outcomes of complexity theory,' says Phipps. And, certainly, this opens up as many creative and speculative avenues (admittedly with some fatalities of unrealistic or illogical conclusions). Nevertheless, it is in such transitional times that new paradigms occur, and it makes one wonder if such fields as ufology are indeed a result—or a symptom—of a worldview increasingly in a state of flux. There is, after all, an '*other* worldview' that is projected from its very premise.

In a sense, what we are coming up against, in a culture breaching the perimeters of its current paradigm, is the recognition of Gödellian incompleteness. The axioms of the past are extending their limits, with the dizzying result of an infinite regress in which the 'conceptual grids' that were firmly set in place begin to disintegrate. This is why Jorjani says that paradigm shifts are rarely rational, for the standard methods of evaluation breakdown and the creation of new models and methods, in their first stages of development, occur out of the flux of 'recombinational delirium'. Rather the emergence from chaos happens in an urgent unification, brought about by circumstances that are testing the paradigm's limits, between two modalities of thinking and perceiving. Indeed, one thinker we shall discuss soon describes a model which corresponds to the transformational potentialities of trauma—echoing the 'chaos' from which new paradigms are birthed.

The problem with modern science, it seems to me, is that it works under the assumption that it is a closed system, and promises—within its own conceptual, axiomatic and epistemological boundaries—an all-encompassing 'theory of everything'. An increasingly disturbing phenomenon is the dogmatic assumption that science, at its present stage of development, has, within its reach, a miraculous key to unlocking all the 'problems' of existence. As Gary Lachman points out, the mysteries, in the eyes of science, are *never* mysterious or wondrous, but become in themselves mere 'problems', which, with the application of logic, will yield to the harsh light of the inquisitor's powers of reason. The problem is of course whether these very assumptions may in themselves obscure, or even ignore altogether, realities, in the form of anomalies, which would precisely expand the spirit of the scientific endeavour for truth, knowledge and insight.

Instead what we are dealing with is not healthy scepticism and intelligent receptiveness to data of great potential importance, but a rigid set of parameters that have turned the enquiring spirit of science into the belief system of *scientism*.[19]

What instead concerns us here is a model which can incorporate, philosophically and cosmologically, what we have already learned from esotericism, psychology, ufology and shamanism. What emerges from all of these subjects is an outline of a radically different reality. A reality, perhaps, that is finally converging precisely at the point where our current paradigms fail to address and integrate.

The metaphor, therefore, of two worlds converging becomes

poignant, for at which point they collide may turn out to be either enhancing or evolutionary; or, if unacknowledged and repressed, dangerously inhibiting to our development. It is also suggestive of *two minds* converging, and one, it seems, may act as a sort of nursling for the other's transition into a new dimension of laws: synchronous rather than causal; metaphoric rather than literal; *meaningful* rather than meaningless; and finally *negentropic* rather than entropic.

Stuart Holroyd, in 'A Sense of Crisis',[20] sums up the direction that we shall take:

> The end of science is to advance knowledge. The primary end of philosophy is not knowledge, but life. Man can do without knowledge, but he cannot do without action. His first need is to live purposively and intensely. *And philosophy, by illuminating the various levels of existence and pointing to its telos or end, enables him to do this* [my italics].

We have already seen that many of the shamanic traditions have a similar method for dealing with incursions of a supernatural nature, particularly with the similarities between the techniques of regression hypnotherapy and the 'Talking Back Ceremony' of the Diné tradition. Both recall memories of anomalous events by placing the subject into a trance. Now, what struck me while reading about the therapeutic techniques deployed in cases of abduction, and particularly a useful component in the transformational process, was a type of exercise developed by the Czech psychologist, Stanislav Grof.

In the late 1950s Grof received a package of the then experimental drug LSD at his offices, where he was working as a psychologist. Grof decided to try the hallucinogenic compound on himself. He was astounded by the meaningful content of the experience. Wilson quotes his experience at length at the beginning of *Alien Dawn*:

I was hit by a radiance that seemed comparable to the light at the epicenter of an atomic explosion... This thunderbolt of light catapulted me from my body... My consciousness seemed to explode into cosmic dimensions.

I found myself thrust into the middle of a cosmic drama that previously had been far beyond even my wildest imaginings. I experienced the Big Bang, raced through black holes and white holes in the universe, my consciousness becoming what could have been exploding supernovas, pulsars, quasars, and other cosmic events. (1999: 2)

Of course the fact that this is reported—rather in the same manner as Ouspensky's experiments with nitrous oxide—after ingesting a mind-altering drug, still nevertheless poses the question of just *why* these extraordinary and apparently cosmic experiences are indeed possible at all. They are not, it seems, random and chaotic, but symbolic, profound and intricate. Indeed, it suggests that the mind has enormous vistas opening before it; providing glimpses into either actual experiences of other realities, or, perhaps, initiating a sort of simulation of cosmogenesis in a vividly symbolic form. Like the other writers and shamans we have discussed in this essay, it provided for Grof what I have called the 'cosmic viewpoint', or recognition, in a sense, of cosmic *telos*.

Grof began as a Freudian, and indeed recognised that Freud had been correct in many respects. For Grof saw that when he administered small doses of LSD to his patients, they vividly relived childhood memories and experiences, along with all the typical traumas which Freud quite correctly identified. However, it was at higher doses, such that Grof himself took, that he realised that the human mind *pans out*, so to speak, and begins to experience semi-religious and mystical states. It was this nature and content of the experience that seemed to suggest to Grof the importance of Jung's notion of the collective unconscious and its archetypal contents and/or realities.

Due to the controversial nature of LSD, and despite its apparently therapeutic benefits when professionally administered, it was eventually deemed illegal for use within the psychiatric establishment. At this point Grof had already relocated to America and had begun to develop a method of breath work which replicated the state of consciousness achieved through LSD dosing; this he called 'holotropic breathing'. Holotropic is a word comprising of two Greek words: *holos*, which means whole, and *trepin*, which means to move in the direction of something—*holotropic*, therefore, means to move in the direction of wholeness.

Now what is interesting about all this is that the extreme and challenging nature of the abduction phenomenon was at first ignored, or wrongly diagnosed, by the medical establishment. There was, prior to more recent times, no framework with which to acknowledge the sheer anomalousness of what was being claimed. Particularly, as it turned out, from individuals that, under further analysis, seemed to be sane and healthy in every other respect.

It was quite natural for a Harvard psychiatrist such as John Mack to seek new models and methodologies within his own profession—ones which might enable a greater understanding of the 'psychological' phenomenon he had agreed to understand—and thus develop a working framework towards a suitable type of therapy. After all, reports of *the abduction experience didn't simply demand a different approach so much as an entirely different set of assumptions about the psyche and the nature of reality.*

The Freudian understanding of an individual unconscious was integrated into the therapeutic process, but what appears to open up in such non-ordinary experiences tended to be a much deeper and collective experience (as can be seen in Grof's description of his vision of cosmic creation). Many of the reductionist models of the psyche, therefore, would tend to unnecessarily pathologise such phenomenon, reducing them to a type of psychosis or a meaningless hallucination. For Mack, however, the holotropic model developed by Grof provided the necessary vocabulary and methodology for grappling with the abduction experience.

Mack required 'an expanded epistemology' that enabled a more holistic approach to these 'neglected aspects of ourselves as instruments of knowing' (1994: 390). He describes the constricting paradigm of reductionist science as being a result of its basic assumptions, that is, its retention, often in the face of facts and reported anomalous experience, of the 'dualistic, subject/object split that characterizes Western empirical science, including psychology' (390). Grof's breath work, then, combined with regression hypnotherapy, for Mack 'became natural investigative allies'. The latter, of course, initiates access into these deeper states of consciousness. Whereas the former acknowledges the *value* of non-ordinary states of consciousness as an access point into deeper levels of psychic—and psychological—realities *beyond everyday consciousness*.

These states, again, open up on to a whole different substrate of existence, and in doing so provide glimpses into the mythological underpinnings which would ordinarily be rejected by more reductionist models. Nevertheless, rationality and reason were of course adhered to firmly: recording data, maintaining scientific discipline and protocol etc., were crucial in creating an atmosphere that was as professional as it was free from unnecessary influences (such as cross-contamination from 'leading' words being said in the hypnotherapy sessions, along with the prevention of biases and so on). The 'alternative' therapies were introduced simply to provide a degree of flexibility in exploring the wide range of emotions and non-ordinary states of consciousness that were fundamental to the abduction experience.

To return back to the UFO phenomenon more generally,

it is a topic that requires a widening of the epistemological presuppositions of reductive science. This accounts for the adoption in many books, including *Alien Dawn*, of a broad and sometimes creative form of speculation which aims to tie-up the loose ends of a phenomenon that fundamentally frustrates the limits of the Western scientific consensus.

Martha Heyneman poetically describes the situation: 'Today, we see rising before us a new shape. We can see its dim outlines through the fog… but we haven't yet come ashore. We don't yet *inhabit* our new picture of the universe' (2001: 18). And when we do inhabit this new cosmology, and we have integrated its laws, we, says Heyneman, 'extrapolate backwards' to provide a new understanding of our origins—individually and cosmically—and where we might be going. In short, it provides us precisely with what the new existentialism sought to prove, and, furthermore, the required knowledge for Holroyd's call for a philosophical basis of evolutionary action.

Now this brings us back nicely to the work of Grof and its philosophical implications as outlined by Richard Tarnas in his book *The Passion of the Western Mind*. For Tarnas the modern reductionist paradigm leaves us adrift in a 'reality that is radically alien to our own, and moreover cannot ever be directly contacted by cognition'. This, he argues, is because of a 'cosmological estrangement of modern consciousness' initiated by Copernicus followed by an ontological one by Descartes and an 'epistemological estrangement initiated by Kant' (2001: 419–420). There is, as a result of this dark triad of estrangement, an existential situation that is along the lines of Wilson's diagnosis in *Beyond the Outsider*:

There is a general feeling that the certainties provided by religion have been lost, and can never be replaced; science, by solving our practical problems, can only make this inner void more painfully obvious. It seems self-evident that in this sense of purpose, inner-direction, Western culture has been running at a heavy loss for at least a hundred years; it is a matter for speculation how long it can go on before becoming completely bankrupt. (1965: 17)

Tarnas similarly lays out a philosophical history to Wilson and provides a similar argument for the recognition of a level of existence composed of an archetypal 'background of values'. These, as we shall see, play a significant role in evolution, particularly in the development of human consciousness. Indeed, Wilson called this underlying meaning of reality 'the information universe' in *Beyond the Occult*. Tarnas, however, begins from the premise that Jung was Freud's true successor in the sense that he went much further with his theory of archetypes, for particularly in his later work, Jung 'began to move toward a conception of archetypes as autonomous patterns of meaning that appear to structure and inhere in both psyche and matter' and thereby 'dissolving the modern subject-object dichotomy' (2001: 425). Again this was Wilson's realisation in *Beyond the Outsider*, for he too asked the question, '... what if science could replace that sense of individual meaning, the feeling of having a direct telephone line to the universal purpose?' (1965: 183).

Now, Jung *had* provided a way of understanding a vast evolutionary source of meaning, and Wilson understood that this was the aim of evolutionary phenomenology, for it can 'change man's conception of himself and of the *interior forces* he has at his command, and ultimately to establish the new evolutionary type, foreshadowed by the "outsiders"' (1965: 183). After all it is the outsider who intuits the limits of his cultural paradigm due to his instinct for an evolutionary system of values from which he can actualise himself. Without these, of course, he becomes a symptom of a sick culture.

If we use Tarnas' analysis we can see that Wilson's 'outsiders' recognise the 'bankruptcy' of values; a world in which the individual is, Tarnas says, at 'once aroused and crushed' in a cosmos that appears inhuman and against, precisely, our own humanity. Wilson describes the situation succinctly in *Introduction to the New Existentialism* (1980): 'Man is alone in an empty universe; no act of his has any meaning outside itself—and its social construct' (152). The world and the universe is a projected machine devoid of purpose, and yet, as Arthur Young pointed out, it's ironic that nobody ever built a machine *without an a priori purpose,* and furthermore, the machine itself, says Rupert Sheldrake, is the ultimate anthropocentric projection of all—a man-made device that is entirely *unnatural!*

The outsider, however, 'is not very concerned with distinction between body and spirit, of man and nature... For him, the only important distinction is between being and nothingness' (1978: 37). In short, Wilson's outsider is in search of *absolutes;* ways through which one can access a direct 'telephone line' to the universal purpose: a psychic link to the vital archetypal forces that underpin the development of consciousness—a sort of evolutionary mysticism. And yet, it is precisely at these binary junctures where man's disconnection to 'universal purpose' appears like huge cracks until he finds himself increasingly relativised, and increasingly *outside.*

The new existentialism was an attempt by Wilson to provide the foundations for an evolutionary phenomenology in which man could access these meaningful levels of reality. Realities that are beyond the ever-increasing relativisms that radically diminish the important role of consciousness. Wilson's recognition of the outsider's plight is based on the distinction of 'Absolute No' versus 'Absolute Yes'; two absolutes. Tarnas describes a similar situation:

> We seem to receive two messages from our existential situation: on the one hand, strive, give oneself to the quest for meaning and spiritual fulfilment; but on the other hand,

know that the universe, of whose substance we are derived, is entirely indifferent to that quest, soulless in character, and nullifying in its effects. (2001: 420)

So what, then, would be the way outside? We can see that the new existentialism and Tarnas seem to be converging upon a solution, offering a phenomenology and a philosophy for advancing mankind's search for meaning.

The archetypes of a culture for Tarnas and Grof have an almost universal origin and are not transcendent or entirely metaphysical. Instead, they are, as they were for Jung, a sort of encoded mythos which captures, usually in symbolic form, the evolutionary trials, tribulations and victories and successes that are echoed throughout *the evolution both biologically and in terms of our consciousness.*

Now, Jordan Peterson admirably summarises Jung's position regarding a culture's paradigms by asking what happens to the 'representational structure in someone's mind (in the human psyche, in human society) when anomalous information, of revolutionary import, is finally accepted as valid?' This question, summarised by Peterson, presents Jung's position:

What happens has a pattern; the pattern has a biological, even genetic basis, which finds its expression in fantasy; such fantasy provides subject material for myth and religion. *The propositions of myth and religion, in turn, help guide and stabilize revolutionary human adaption* [my italics]. (1999: 405)

Contrasting with Peterson's summary we may also include the essentially *destabilizing* archetype of the trickster figure, with the UFO following not far behind.

Now, UFO entities, as we have seen in Jorjani's recognition that their intentions seem to 'sink into… the mythic folklore of a culture', present a disturbing number of problems. Jorjani concludes in favour of a very thoroughgoing phenomenological as well as scientific analysis of the subject to prevent a potentially dangerous shift in the public perception towards cults and an anti-scientific religion aided by these cosmic tricksters. This is along the same lines as Jacques Vallée's *Messengers of Deception*, which Wilson felt was a 'step backward into conspiracy theories' (1999: 134), and yet these realities, insofar as they occur in misguided beliefs and dangerous cults, indeed *do* make up a part of the developing UFO mythos.

The fault may lie fundamentally in the belief that all experiences are uniform and under control by the same entities—and some may be archetypal manifestations of the deviant trickster—that 'dialectical antagonist' who works to challenge, subvert, obscure and to fool—with a goal that is essentially enigmatic and mercurial by definition.

Harpur indeed notes that hoaxes usually aim to 'expose some flaw in society', and, 'There is a sinister aspect to all hoaxers. They play god behind the scenes' (2003: 167). These 'scenes' seem to be played out upon and within human consciousness. Their origin, and often symbolism, appears to be archetypal and in some cases heuristic. One gets the sense that there is an almost Socratic urgency behind it all to 'Know Thyself', their aim being, as Wilson suggests, is like any good teacher: 'by making the pupil *want* to learn' and to 'lure free will into expressing itself and its own existence' (1999: 337). The transformational results, as we have seen, confirm a multidimensional as well as profound recognition that it is *us*, in the end, who are masters of our own destiny. Indeed, it is very rare that these entities make promises, and if they do, they are usually symbolical and rarely fulfilled.

There is the sense that they are saying, like Wilson's character in *The Mind Parasites*: 'Nothing could be more dangerous for the human race than to believe that its affairs had fallen into the hands of supermen.'

This brief digression into the murkier areas of archetypes,

particularly the trickster figure and its deceptions, has been necessary simply to acknowledge the problems of an undisciplined approach to archetypal forces. Jorjani, like Grof, recognises the substrate of powerful evolutionary forces that are anything but passive. And great care must be taken, with the aid of reason and, indeed, precisely the archetypal forces—availed by science—that counteract the 'psychological warfare' by recognising the familiar 'calling cards of the archetypal trickster' (2016: xliv). Science itself, for Jorjani, is powered by archetypal forces embodied in such archetypes as Prometheus and Atlas.

Now, with each paradigm there is, implicit within it, a lifespan, for such a metaphor or model can only last as long as it remains a practical model of reality, and after that, the anomalies eventually flood in overwhelmingly. Rather like metaphors themselves, as Bernardo Kastrup argues convincingly, we must treat them as 'disposable vehicles' rather than adhere to them too preciously. But we may instead, he continues, use them 'to describe a new idea gestalt'. Importantly, he concludes, 'Once this essential meaning is conveyed, one must discard the vehicle as if it were disposable packaging, lest it outlive its usefulness and turn into an intellectual entrapment.' This, of course, has been the essential message of this essay, and it is also captured in Goethe's *Faust*:

All that doth pass away
Is but a symbol.

And yet, with each passing symbol there is an often-traumatic transitional period that births a new, more substantial, symbol to account for the limitations of the old one.

Grof's work provides the link between the symbolic and evolutionary metaphoric worlds, and the material and biological world of human experience. He does so, Tarnas explains, by providing 'a more explicit biological ground to the Jungian archetypes, while giving a more explicit archetypal ground to the Freudian instincts'. Much of the archetypal imagery that occurs in Jung's analysis is obviously drawn from religion, story, and mythology and so on, and further still it exists in a collective unconscious.

Now Jung concludes his excellent essay, 'Approaching the Unconscious', by saying that: 'Our actual knowledge of the unconscious shows that it is a natural phenomenon and that, like Nature herself, it is at least *neutral*. It contains all aspects of human nature—light and dark, beautiful and ugly, good and evil, profound and silly.' In short what Jung is suggesting is that the unconsciousness is connected with the symbolic forces at the heart of Nature, that it is, as a product of natural forces, an expression of its tremendously complex dynamism—a force that births new and evermore complex forms into existence.

The archetypes for Grof are in a strange position *between* birth and death, which as Tarnas describes, becomes 'a kind of transduction point between dimensions, a pivot that linked the biological and archetypal, the Freudian and the Jungian, the biographical and collective, the personal and the transpersonal, body and spirit' (2001: 428). What happens in Groffian therapy is an experiential reliving of the traumas of being born, the very moments we first arrive into existence, and, indeed, right back *before* we exist, that is, up until the point of our apparent *pre-existent annihilation*. Grof's own vision of a cosmic destruction and rebirth as experienced under the influence of LSD seems to be a symbolic representation of this same process. Essentially what happens after such experiences is a radical transformation—an ontological shift—in which the individual's sense of disconnection with the archetypal forces of existence is wedded together in a form of 'participation mystique'.

Our usual dismissal of the psychological realities of the birth process, Grof and Tarnas argue, is the reason why Western civilization has increasingly become dualistic, making sharp distinctions between man and nature, real and unreal, and so on. As we have seen, this breaks down in Ouspensky's experience as well as with the shamanic initiation ceremonies and other mystical insights. Indeed, here we may turn to the epistemologist, Jean Piaget, and expand its content to include Grof's conclusions:

> Knowledge does not begin in the I, and it does not begin in the object; it begins in the interactions... then there is a reciprocal and simultaneous construction of the subject on the one hand and the object on the other. (1999: 409)

One is here reminded of Julian Jaynes' auditory hallucination which contained the phrase: 'Include the knower in the known'. This led him to write his famous book, *The Origin of Consciousness in the Breakdown of the Bicameral Mind*, which argued of a split-brain schism in ancient man that birthed the modern self-reflective consciousness. The 'old' consciousness was participatory but at the expense of our sense of individuality as we understand it today. Nevertheless, there may have been, in a sense, an archetypal *impetus* for this expulsion from the womb-like seamlessness of 'self and other' which led to the rapid development of an individualized ego consciousness.

The abductee 'Jerry' provides a beatifically poetic and metaphorical allegory for this process of the expulsion and resulting differentiation of consciousness—and, significantly, its *return*:

> Imagine that your essence, your soul, was part of a whole, and as part of a whole you decided to give birth, to create. You then gave birth to your thought to create and made your thought into matter. As this birth came to be solid, you then decided you would continue to create, and after some time you decided you would like to be whole again. But in order

to be whole again you had to gather up all of the fragments or pieces of your whole being. In order to become whole again you must be able to then understand that you have to then create and give birth to that thought. And in order to go back to your original form you must again reverse the process. (1994: 141)

What makes 'Jerry's' description so interesting is its holistic and evolutionary theme of development throughout the varying stages of disconnection, dis-integration and the yearning to return to wholeness. Furthermore, it suggests a creative dynamic which, in the initiation of creation itself, the individual becomes precisely that: an individualized ego consciousness. But, at some crucial junction in the span of his or her life, they may awaken to their predicament—they become existentially self-aware and feel themselves to be disconnected from their once entranced and illusory existence. Intransigence and contingency appear for them as an insurmountable *fact* of human existence, and this devalues the entire foundation of their Being. And unless this individual takes solace in religion or, like Sartre, pursues a political vision for the emancipation of mankind through social justice, then this individual is left with the profoundly shaking realisation that demands of them a far more universal sense of ultimate values, of a foundational *cosmic meaning* that is experientially felt, not simply intellectually 'understood'.

In short, the individual becomes Wilson's outsider, and requires a positive existentialism which can unify these inner conflicts, and provide a bridge towards a more integrated sense of his existence.

In terms of the new existentialism, it is precisely at this point of existential revelation that we truly ask the question of 'Who am I?', and it is also, in a sense, the same point we begin to 'yearn for wholeness'—consciously or unconsciously—of which 'Jerry' refers to. Wilson says that these represent the 'very outer reaches of consciousness', a point where one '"wakes up" to a sense of the total absurdity of his position in the restricted world of ordinary consciousness' (1980: 118).

In Grof's analysis this would be the 'Expulsion from Paradise' phase of the perinatal experience in which one reaches the transitional stage of environmental threat, and undergoes simultaneous death and rebirth. What's more, Grof notes the existential echoes of this experience in many of the works of art and philosophies developed by such existentialists as Sartre, Camus and Soren Kierkegaard. Existence for them has become a toxic closed-system in which there is no escape but through death or delusion. Grof, who initiated these experiences through LSD both on himself and his patients, noted that this reliving of this stage produced in some 'a deep connection with existential philosophy' which embodies the sense of 'hopelessness and absurdity of this state'; indeed it is in this state of moral and spiritual entrapment, archetypally represented in the transition stage of birth in the constricting environment of the cervix, that is encapsulated in the title of Sartre's famous play, *No Exit*.

Grof continues: 'An important influence on Sartre's life was a difficult and poorly resolved session with the psychedelic substance, mescaline.' Significantly Wilson summarises Sartre's philosophy by saying that everything else is 'blocked', with the exception of commitment to socialist politics, and his philosophy became a 'closed subject, for there is no point in thinking further; we shall only keep returning to the recognition that all roads are blocked but this one' (1990: 53). For Sartre and many others who accept the ultimate conclusions of existentialism, there is no 'way outside'. No escape.

And yet, for Wilson there is a way out of this fundamentally transitional stage, and these are often experienced in non-ordinary states of consciousness, in glimpses of Faculty X and peak experiences. He continues to say that man realises this in 'moments when he becomes aware that he contains a "god-like" chaos, that he is potentially an enormous force.' These moments, of course, are the opposite of Sartre's sense of limitedness, and infer a far greater reality, a rebirth in fact, into an open system of *relational* values and sheer meaningfulness—even a new paradigm and a whole new sense of reality itself. '[For] in nausea man feels isolated in an alien world of objects; in the moments of insight, he becomes aware of a connection between himself and nature—that he is capable of a meaningful relationship with nature' (1965: 160). His consciousness becomes *participatory* rather than solipsistic and suffocating in its own self-imposed limitations.

All of this, of course, can be interpreted on many levels and, in the context of this essay, provides the analogy of existing between two worlds, psychologically and cosmologically—the mind and reality.

Now, this sort of intentional bridging between man and nature, psyche and cosmos, and so on, is wonderfully described by Ouspensky when he says, in his essay 'Superman', that 'Man is a little universe'. He continues:

In him proceed *continual death and continual rebirth*... And the desire of God in man, that is, *the directing forces of his spirit, conscious of its own unity with the infinite consciousness of the universe*, cannot be in harmony... with the 'three dimensional' consciousness of man, *which is based on his separating himself from the world*, on his opposing to the world his own 'I' and on *his recognising the reality of all apparent forms and divisions*. (1989: 118)

Again what Ouspensky seems to be suggesting is essentially the recognition that man, in Wilson's terms, has the potential for 'god-like chaos', or, within us, we have the capacity for leaping across the apparent chasm between ourselves and the cosmos and, in doing so, understanding our psychic capacity for affirming existence and of our role in its greatest revealing of meaning and evolutionary intentionality. Man's future evolution, Wilson writes, 'depends upon an increased ability to use "intentions"', however, these 'intentions do not create ideas or insights; they only *uncover* meaning.' This, of course, is in direct contrast to Sartre's solipsism which understands all meanings to be entirely mind-generated illusions that refer essentially only to a meaningless chaos, a reality that is fundamentally impersonal, even somewhat hostile to man's goals with its sheer inhuman neutrality. This, of course, is the world modern man finds himself in and which Tarnas so eloquently describes.

Ouspensky similarly expresses this 'god-like' component within human beings, and like Grof he calls it a tropism, 'the directing forces of his spirit', a tendency, in other words, towards wholeness. This tendency, which simultaneously pushes us forward also, paradoxically, differentiates us, for our consciousness, blinkered as it often is, shuts out more than it lets in. And yet, despite this disconnection, becomes in moments altogether integrated and whole, and is further aided by Wilson's recognition of a way outside the entrapments of pessimism and solipsism, for consciousness, as he says, *reveals meanings which have a substantially objective existence.* Indeed, Wilson concludes in *New Pathways of Psychology*:

> We are living in a world of infinitely rich meaning and we possess the equipment for 'playing it back.' The chief obstacle is our ignorance of the purpose of the equipment and the meaning waiting to be decoded. (1990: in Dossor: 112)

There is the sense that there are meanings that animate the deepest substratum of existence, and that, in some odd way, these meanings are the structural blueprints not only of matter and the physical and natural world, but also the structuring forces that underlie experience as well as existence in its interior and mental form. The mind, then, is just as much a part of this reality of objective meanings as it is capable of unveiling or *revealing* them. In fact, it is essentially revealing deeper layers of its connection to reality itself, and, as a result, there is the sense of unity consciousness and an overcoming of the Sartrean kind of existential alienation. More than this is the direct access to information or unusual powers which, as we have seen, are exhibited by the UFO entities and many of the abductees themselves.

Whitley Strieber, who has had multiple such experiences with these beings, has also noted a similar convergence of worlds, not only between causal and synchronous existence, physical and non-physical, but also between the living and the dead. He uses much the same language as others we have explored; for example in discussing the near-death experience he notes, much like the shamans, that those who undergo these intense states become 'the wonder workers of modern times, leading us into an entirely new understanding of and relationship with our own souls.' Strieber continues:

> Their reports suggest that the soul is not only real, but that what we think of as reality is actually a small corner of a much larger world. *They suggest that consciousness is not only in us and part of us, but more that we are in consciousness, journeying through a world largely unseen by us in bodies that appear to be designed to filter out any vision of the larger reality* [my italics]. (2017: 89)

Again, there is the simultaneous recognition of the existence of such an objective reality of meaning, *and* the recognition that our bodies filter such information out for the sake of our evolution—the 'reducing valve'. However, these UFO entities, or 'visitors' as Strieber calls them, appear to be somehow involved in the transition and transformation between two worlds. And that, in a sense, many of the individuals who undergo such experiences become the Western equivalent of the shaman, an individual who is able to walk between these two worlds. Strangely, but nonetheless profound in its implications, is Strieber's claim for continued communication with his dead wife, Anne Strieber, and furthermore her response when Whitley enquired about the role of these visitors. Indeed, this provides an interesting clue regarding their baffling presence. She describes them as 'inner beings', and that they 'live within reality. You're on the surface.' Whitley continues to say that the entities themselves aided in this communication with his deceased wife, and that they have taught them to live as a whole species 'with the physical and nonphysical sides in contact,' and furthermore this presages 'the next stage in evolution' (2017: 26).

It is this notion that the role of much unusual phenomena is essentially heuristic, it is teaching and bridging between two worlds. Strieber's example pulls together many of the threads explored throughout this essay. And, furthermore, the sheer seamlessness of the new existentialism runs throughout, showing us not only the potential powers of human consciousness but opening the doors for the exploration of entire new realities. What it provides is a phenomenological analysis of these limitations of our body-as-receiver, and the recognition of a much wider reality that far exceeds our ordinary understanding of reality. It represents the turning point from existential entrapment in the phenomenal world to the experiential affirmation of meanings that are a fundamental part of our Being.

The new existentialism enriches the reading and understanding of much occult and paranormal literature, for it provides a practical framework for their integration. And if these visitors are indeed here to bridge two worlds, from the inside out, one might then turn to the work of Colin Wilson as one of the crucial moments when we, from *this side*, began to recognise a new world awaiting within our own consciousness.

In fact, in this last section I have attempted to run along several complementary theories of human nature, from the ancient practices of shamanism to the philosophical implications of the abduction phenomenon. The work of Grof and Tarnas, I feel, has also provided a large-scale context for us to understand the birth pangs of a new paradigm emerging out of the shell of the old one. What, essentially, these brief explorations into new models of reality has provided is a potential mapping of the world that Wilson intuited in his earliest works. The inner dimension of the UFO is not so much esoteric as a 'living hieroglyph', a symbol or an existential challenge, that provides a curious glimpse into another order of logic that is analogical and heuristic, a teaching from these 'inner beings'.

What I have hoped to achieve with this essay is a panoramic view of a world of meanings and evolutionary potentialities as they are hinted at in the literature of ufology. Wilson's approach to existentialism in his earliest books to his later works on the occult and UFOs all naturally grew out of this deep recognition that there *is* far more to life, and in Strieber's case, even to death. Increasingly as one reads through the case studies and testimony one is reminded of the essential message of Wilson's philosophy, and this provides a much-needed re-evaluation of our reductionist culture. One gets the sense that much like Wilson said of Goethe's *Faust*, the 'longing for the "occult" is the instinctive desire to believe in the unseen forces, the wider significances, that can break the circuit' (1988: 25). Ufology provides much the same stimulus and attraction as the occult, and provides a means of widening man's sense of significance and wider meanings.

Of course, a sceptic would say that this is mere immaturity, an invalid and futile attempt to supplement reality for the comfort of fantasy and delusion. And yet this doesn't seem to be the case, for often these experiences with the UFO are often deeply traumatic and *then proceed afterwards to grow into a profound and deeply seated sense of increasing significance and a widened sense of possibility.* Wilson continues in *The Occult* to say that: 'Man lives and evolves by "eating" significance,' and that the 'deeper his sense of wonder, the wider his curiosity, the stronger his vitality becomes, and the more powerful his grip on his own existence' (1988: 26). Therefore this sort of meaningful investigation into the stranger mysteries such as the UFO represents need not be an exercise in delusion, but as an exercise in phenomenology, and a valid attempt to understand an aspect of reality that is too often undeservedly ignored. The phenomenon itself seems to be attempting to teach us something about our reality, and it certainly benefits us to know precisely what that might be.

The UFO, like the occult, becomes a poignant symbol of inner transformation, and rather than simply being a field of inner knowledge of the unseen, the UFO appears to be an entirely *seen* phenomenon, and seems to infer another realm of Being and beings. It is the occult radically *seen*. It is, in a sense, the occult world made manifest, a curious reminder of our state of spiritual neglect that presents itself as a difficult and archetypally-charged Zen kōan. Waiting, it seems, our enlightenment until it provides its full import. 'We *have* to learn to expand inward until we have somehow re-established the sense of *huaca* [life force], until we have recreated the feeling of "unseen forces" ... It has somehow *got* to be done,' says Wilson. The UFO is urging us to do just that. And like most of occult significances and symbols, they refer to an inner reality, and that it is in the mind of the occult practitioner where the realities of both worlds unite. And eventually these metaphors and synchronicities incorporate themselves into our everyday lives and cease to be unreal, but as important indicators of our very real purpose.

These 'unseen forces' appear to *live through us*, and its language is suited towards wonder and the symbolic. And it is the evolutionary metaphor, that symbol of potential from the inner worlds, that urges us to actualise it into reality. If, as Grof and Wilson suggest, these UFO entities are as 'in-between' as they appear, then their often-symbolic content and communications may presage a new relationship towards our own consciousness.

The new existentialism and the UFO are not as far apart from each other as one might think. *Alien Dawn*, an exploration of the many facets of the phenomenon, advances our deeper understanding into the unusual and powerful forces that urge us to bridge two worlds. Wilson provided the intellectual and spiritual tools necessary to navigate these new territories within the evolutionary mind—both our own and our mysterious visitors from inner-space...

References

Barrett, W. (1990) *Irrational Man: A Study in Existential Philosophy*. US: Anchor Books.

Bassett, M. (1995) *Author's Emendations to The New Existentialism*. California: Private Publishing.

Bergson, H. (2014) *Creative Evolution*. New York: Dover Publications, Inc.

Blavatsky, HB (2012) *Abridgement of the Secret Doctrine*. London: Quest Books.

Carroll, P. (2008) *The Apophenion: A Chaos Magick Paradigm*. Oxford: Mandrake.

Carroll, P. (2011) *The Octavo*. Oxford: Mandrake.

Connor, N. & Keeney, B. (eds.) (2008) *Shamans of the World*. Boulder, CO: Sounds True, Inc.

Daumal, R. (2004) *Mount Analogue*. London: Overlook Press.

Dick, PK (1996) *The Shifting Realities of Philip K. Dick: Selected Literary and Philosophical Writings*. New York: Random House USA Inc.

Dossor, H. (1990) *Colin Wilson: The Man & His Mind*. Dorset: Element Books Ltd.

Gettings, F. (1989) *The Secret Lore of the Cat*. Carol Publishing Group.

Gooch, S. (1978) *The Paranormal*. London: HarperCollins.

Gooch, S. (1980) *The Double Helix of the Mind*. London: Wildwood House.

Harpur, P. (2003) *Daimonic Reality: A Field Guide to the Otherworld*. Enumclaw, Washington: Pine Winds Press.

Heyneman, M. (2001) *The Breathing Cathedral: Feeling Our Way Into a Living Cosmos*. Indiana: iUniverse.

Hitchens, P. (2010) *The Rage Against God*. London: Continuum Publishing Corporation.

Holmes, R. (1982) *Coleridge*. Oxford: Oxford University Press.

Hyde, L. (2008) *Trickster Makes This World: Mischief, Myth and Art.* Edinburgh: Canongate Books.

James, W. (1909) 'Final Impressions of a Psychical Researcher' (originally 'The Confidences of a "psychical researcher"', *American Magazine*, October 1909).

Jorjani, JR (2016) *Prometheus and Atlas.* Budapest: Arktos.

Jung, CG (1990) *The Undiscovered Self.* Princeton, NJ: Princeton University Press.

Jung, CG (1995) *Memories, Dreams, Reflections.* London: Fontana Press.

Jung, CG (2002) *Flying Saucers: A Modern Myth of Things Seen in the Sky.* London: Routledge.

Koestler, A. (1966) *The Act of Creation.* London: Pan Books Ltd.

Kripal, J. (2010) *Authors of the Impossible: The Paranormal and the Sacred.* Chicago: University of Chicago Press.

Lachman, G. (2013) *The Caretakers of the Cosmos: Living Responsibly in an Unfinished World.* Edinburgh: Floris Books.

Lachman, G. (2015) *The Secret Teachers of the Western World.* New York: Jeremy P. Tarcher/Penguin.

Lachman, G. (2016) *Beyond the Robot: The Life and Work of Colin Wilson.* New York: Jeremy P. Tarcher/Penguin.

Lachman, G. (2017) *Lost Knowledge of the Imagination.* Edinburgh: Floris Books.

Mack, J. (1994) *Abduction: Human Encounters with Aliens.* Glasgow: Simon & Schuster.

McGilchrist, I. (2012) *The Master and his Emissary.* London: Yale University Press.

Miłosz, Czesław (1982) *Visions from San Francisco Bay.* New York: Farrar, Straus & Giroux.

Nicoll, M. (1976) *Living Time and the Integration of the Life.* Boulder, CO: Shambhala Publications, Inc.

Ouspensky, PD (1989) *A New Model of the Universe.* London: Arkana.

Ouspensky, PD (2001) *In Search of the Miraculous.* New York:

Harcourt, Inc.

Peterson, J. (1999) *Maps of Meaning: The Architecture of Belief.* London: Routledge.

Peterson, J. (1999) *Maps of Meaning: The Architecture of Belief.* New York: Routledge.

Phipps, C. (2012) *Evolutionaries.* New York: Harper Perennial.

Puharich, A. (1974) *Uri: A journal of the mystery of Uri Geller.* US: Anchor Press.

Reeve, B. (1965) *The Advent of the Cosmic Viewpoint.* US: Amherst.

Roberts, Adam (2016) *The Thing Itself.* London: Gollancz.

Spurgeon, B. (2006) *Colin Wilson: Philosopher of Optimism.* Michael Butterworth.

Stanley, C. (2016) *An Evolutionary Leap: Colin Wilson on Psychology.* London: Karnac Books.

Stanley, C. (ed.) (2017) *Proceedings of the First International Colin Wilson Conference.* Newcastle upon Tyne: Cambridge Scholars Publishing.

Strieber, W. (1988) *Transformation.* London: Arrow Books Ltd.

Strieber, W. (2012) *Solving the Communion Enigma.* London: Penguin Group.

Strieber, W. & Kripal, JJ (2016) *The Super Natural.* New York: Jeremy P. Tarcher.

Strieber, W. & Strieber, A. (2017) *The Afterlife Revolution.* Walker & Collier, Inc.

Talbot, M. (1991) *Mysticism and the New Physics.* London: Penguin.

Tarnas, R. (2001) *The Passion of the Western Mind.* London: Pimlico.

Turner, K. (2016) *Sky Shamans of Mongolia.* Berkeley, CA: North Atlantic Books.

Vallée, JF (1975) *Passport to Magonia: From Folklore to Flying Saucers.* London: Tandem Books.

Vallée, JF (2014) *The Invisible College: What a Group of Scientists Has Discovered About UFO Influence on the Human Race.* Charlottesville: Anomalist Books.

Watson, I. (2003) *Miracle Visitors.* London: Gollancz.

Watson, L. (1976) *Gifts of Unknown Things*. London: Hodder & Stoughton Ltd.

Wilson, C. (1965) *Beyond the Outsider: A Philosophy of the Future*. London: Pan Books Ltd.

Wilson, C. (1966) *Introduction to the New Existentialism*. Boston: Houghton Mifflin Company.

Wilson, C. (1970) *Origins of the Sexual Impulse*. London: Granada Publishing Limited.

Wilson, C. (1973) *Strange Powers*. London: Latimer New Dimensions Ltd.

Wilson, C. (1978) *The Outsider*. London: Pan Books Ltd.

Wilson, C. (1979) *Mysteries*. London: Grafton.

Wilson, C. (1980) *Starseekers*. London: Hodder & Stoughton Ltd.

Wilson, C. (1980) *The New Existentialism*. London: Wildwood House Ltd.

Wilson, C. (1985) *The Essential Colin Wilson*. London: Harrap Limited.

Wilson, C. (1988) *The Occult*. London: Grafton Books.

Wilson, C. (1989) *Existentially Speaking: Essays on the Philosophy of Literature*. California: Borgo Press.

Wilson, C. (1990) *Religion and The Rebel*. London: Ashgrove Publishing Ltd.

Wilson, C. (1998) *The Books in My Life*. Charlottesville: Hampton Roads Publishing Company, Inc.

Wilson, C. (1999) *Alien Dawn: An Investigation into the Contact Experience*. London: Virgin Books.

Wilson, C. (2005) *World Famous UFOs*. London: Constable and Robinson.

Wilson, C. (2008) *Beyond the Occult*. London: Watkins Publishing.

Wilson, C. (2009) *Super Consciousness: The Quest for the Peak Experience*. London: Watkins Publishing.

Endnotes

1. There is also, of course, the 'nuts-and-bolts' interpretation that says it is *entirely* an objective phenomenon—a craft from out of space full of real, living and breathing creatures. Yet, much of the literature suggests that this is not entirely the case.

2. https://isthisanything.org/2014/08/17/pareidolia-in-art-quote-from-leonardo-da-vinci/

3. Values—conveyed by creation, natural or man-made—of course, are different. Love, for example, exists in the world of values, the atmosphere in which our emotional 'culture' thrives.

4. The philosopher Alfred North Whitehead called this 'causal efficacy' which Wilson translated into the more understandable 'meaning perception'. For a full clarification, see Wilson's *Beyond the Outsider* (1965).

5. Sceptics declare that there is absolutely no reality to the phenomenon whatsoever; or, for that matter, that it can be explained away as misidentified aircraft, weather balloons, or sightings or secretive military technology undisclosed to the public. None of this can be entirely discounted of course, yet an honest reading of ufological literature raises too many questions—and these reductive answers diminish a complex phenomenon to a simple, comfortable 'explanation'. The chief difficulty in studies such as this is to sift through the evidence and maintain an unbiased sense of discrimination. Furthermore, there is the uncomfortable problem of temporarily jettisoning firmly-held beliefs, for the phenomenon does not cater for our ordinary understanding of reality, and this, it could be said, argues in favour of the sceptic's justifiable sense of exasperation.

   The sceptic, moreover, hedges his bets: for is it really

worth investigating a phenomenon that may turn out to be little more than a giant hoax, or misidentification? This is an entirely sympathetic position, for most of us have lives that are already complex and difficult enough, and to pursue this apparently impossible subject becomes a question of its 'existential component': for what, in fact, does one expect to gain? One could even say that it is less about closed-mindedness than a means of preserving intellectual energy and integrity. A necessary type of economical use of one's time in the face of often exhausting and inconclusive information. If the cultural climate tends to dismiss it as trivial nonsense, it might be enough for one to disregard the subject. Again, this is basically a healthy enough reaction, and one can be sympathetic.

6. https://www.youtube.com/watch?v=wAY1YX1h49E
7. http://www.compilerpress.ca/Competitiveness/Anno/ Anno%20Heidegger%20The%20Age%20of%20the%20 World%20Picture.htm
8. http://www.ianwatson.info/farewell-colin-wilson/
9. http://adsabs.harvard.edu/full/1986QJRAS..27...94D
10. https://totalgooch.wordpress.com/bibliography/1981- science-fiction-as-religion-with-christopher-evans-brans- head-books-ltd/full-essay/
11. http://www.ralphmag.org/EB/godboles-song.html
12. https://jordanbpeterson.com/bible-series/
13. In a short series of books by Jeremy Naydler called *Technology and the Soul* (2010) he examines how logic has been transferred to the domain of the machine— and although human beings still obviously use logic, it is nevertheless radically diminished by this reliance on computers and other devices. Naydler argues that this sort of 'calculative thinking' in the Middle Ages was called ratio. In this bestowing on machines our own ability for ratio, we have, he argues, grown a 'collective ratio' that has 'grown

far more powerful through its having been, in a certain one-sided way, embodied in machines. And so the influence of the ratio on the whole psychic and spiritual makeup of the human being is far greater today than it has ever been.' Naydler goes on to warn us that the 'danger that faces us is that we all become so mesmerized by the brilliance of our computers that we begin to think like them, and forget what it means to think humanly.' (19)

14. https://www.newdawnmagazine.com/articles/aliens-predictions-the-secret-school-decoding-the-work-of-whitley-strieber

15. http://disinfo.com/2014/10/pop-magic-grant-morrison/

16. From Colin Wilson's 'Whitehead as Existentialist': https://philosophynow.org/issues/64/Whitehead_As_Existentialist

17. http://www.allaboutheaven.org/observations/9034/221/daumal-rene-a-fundamental-experiment-part-1-011120

18. I first became aware of the idea of 'creative resonance' in a 2003 interview with the science-fiction writer, Roberto Quaglia, who describes it as when 'a metaphoric child is born... which is a new concept which could have operated in a moment or not, or become a new philosophy': https://youtu.be/29f1ho_Io48?t=44m27s

19. Now it is not my intention to go into any great depth regarding the philosophical and psychological problems—or mysteries—that exist within establishment science, for there are many more qualified critics, often scientists themselves, that have succeeded—in my mind—at unravelling and addressing these self-limiting assumptions. Rupert Sheldrake's *The Science Delusion* is perhaps the most formidable book on the subject, whereas a philosophical argument for a different emphasis regarding the spirit of our *attention* to the natural world has been convincingly argued in EF Schumacher's book, *A Guide for the Perplexed.*

20. https://www.counter-currents.com/2015/03/a-sense-of-crisis/

BOOKS

O-BOOKS

SPIRITUALITY

O is a symbol of the world, of oneness and unity; this eye represents knowledge and insight. We publish titles on general spirituality and living a spiritual life. We aim to inform and help you on your own journey in this life.

If you have enjoyed this book, why not tell other readers by posting a review on your preferred book site? Recent bestsellers from O-Books are:

Heart of Tantric Sex

Diana Richardson

Revealing Eastern secrets of deep love and intimacy to Western couples.

Paperback: 978-1-90381-637-0 ebook: 978-1-84694-637-0

Crystal Prescriptions

The A-Z guide to over 1,200 symptoms and their healing crystals

Judy Hall

The first in the popular series of six books, this handy little guide is packed as tight as a pill-bottle with crystal remedies for ailments.

Paperback: 978-1-90504-740-6 ebook: 978-1-84694-629-5

Take Me To Truth
Undoing the Ego
Nouk Sanchez, Tomas Vieira
The best-selling step-by-step book on shedding the Ego, using the
teachings of *A Course In Miracles*.
Paperback: 978-1-84694-050-7 ebook: 978-1-84694-654-7

The 7 Myths about Love...Actually!
The journey from your HEAD to the HEART of your SOUL
Mike George
Smashes all the myths about LOVE.
Paperback: 978-1-84694-288-4 ebook: 978-1-84694-682-0

The Holy Spirit's Interpretation of the New Testament
A course in Understanding and Acceptance
Regina Dawn Akers
Following on from the strength of *A Course In Miracles*, NTI
teaches us how to experience the love and oneness of God.
Paperback: 978-1-84694-085-9 ebook: 978-1-78099-083-5

The Message of A Course In Miracles
A translation of the text in plain language
Elizabeth A. Cronkhite
A translation of *A Course in Miracles* into plain, everyday
language for anyone seeking inner peace. The companion
volume, *Practicing A Course In Miracles*, offers practical lessons
and mentoring.
Paperback: 978-1-84694-319-5 ebook: 978-1-84694-642-4

Thinker's Guide to God
Peter Vardy
An introduction to key issues in the philosophy of religion.
Paperback: 978-1-90381-622-6

Your Simple Path
Find happiness in every step
Ian Tucker
A guide to helping us reconnect with what is really important in our lives.
Paperback: 978-1-78279-349-6 ebook: 978-1-78279-348-9

365 Days of Wisdom
Daily Messages To Inspire You Through The Year
Dadi Janki
Daily messages which cool the mind, warm the heart and guide you along your journey.
Paperback: 978-1-84694-863-3 ebook: 978-1-84694-864-0

Body of Wisdom
Women's Spiritual Power and How it Serves
Hilary Hart
Bringing together the dreams and experiences of women across the world with today's most visionary spiritual teachers.
Paperback: 978-1-78099-696-7 ebook: 978-1-78099-695-0

Dying to Be Free
From Enforced Secrecy to Near Death to True Transformation
Hannah Robinson
After an unexpected accident and near-death experience, Hannah Robinson found herself radically transforming her life, while a remarkable new insight altered her relationship with her father, a practising Catholic priest.
Paperback: 978-1-78535-254-6 ebook: 978-1-78535-255-3

The Ecology of the Soul
A Manual of Peace, Power and Personal Growth for Real People
in the Real World
Aidan Walker
Balance your own inner Ecology of the Soul to regain your
natural state of peace, power and wellbeing.
Paperback: 978-1-78279-850-7 ebook: 978-1-78279-849-1

Not I, Not other than I
The Life and Teachings of Russel Williams
Steve Taylor, Russel Williams
The miraculous life and inspiring teachings of one of the World's
greatest living Sages.
Paperback: 978-1-78279-729-6 ebook: 978-1-78279-728-9

On the Other Side of Love
A Woman's Unconventional Journey Towards Wisdom
Muriel Maufroy
When life has lost all meaning, what do you do?
Paperback: 978-1-78535-281-2 ebook: 978-1-78535-282-9

Practicing A Course In Miracles
A Translation of the Workbook in Plain Language and With
Mentoring Notes
Elizabeth A. Cronkhite
The practical second and third volumes of The Plain-Language
A Course In Miracles.
Paperback: 978-1-84694-403-1 ebook: 978-1-78099-072-9